Straight Talk About Anxiety and Depression

Straight Talk About Anxiety and Depression

Michael Maloney, M.D.,
and
Rachel Kranz

 Facts On File

New York • Oxford

Straight Talk About Anxiety and Depression
Copyright © 1991 by Elizabeth A. Ryan

Facts On File, Inc.
460 Park Avenue South
New York NY 10016
USA

Facts On File Limited
c/o Roundhouse Publishing Ltd.
P.O. Box 140
Oxford OX2 7SF
United Kingdom

Library of Congress Cataloging-in-Publication Data
Maloney, Michael, 1944–
    Straight talk about anxiety and depression / by Michael Maloney, M.D., and Rachel Kranz.
        p. cm.
    Includes index.
    Summary: Discusses the different types of stress that can affect teenagers, the anxiety and depression that may result, and ways of coping with these situations.
    ISBN 0-8160-2434-0
    1. Stress in adolescence—Juvenile literature. 2. Anxiety in adolescence—Juvenile literature. 3. Depression in adolescence—Juvenile literature. 4. Teenagers—Mental health services—Juvenile literature. [1. Stress (Psychology) 2. Anxiety. 3. Depression. Mental.]   I. Kranz, Rachel. II. Title.
    BF724.3.S86S67 1991
    155.5'18—dc20   90-23858

A British CIP data available on request from Facts On File.

Facts On File books are available at special discounts when purchased in bulk quantities for businesses, associations, institutions or sales promotions. Please contact the Special Sales Department of our New York office at 212/683-2244 (dial 800/322-8755 except in NY, AK or HI).

Text design by Catherine Hyman
Jacket design by Catherine Hyman
Composition by Facts On File, Inc.
Manufactured by the Maple-Vail Book Manufacturing Group
Printed in the United States of America

10 9 8 7 6 5 4 3 2

This book is printed on acid-free paper.

Contents

1

Teenage
Pressures

Cassie's parents are going through a messy divorce. Two months ago, her father moved out and now her mother can't even mention his name without getting angry. They're fighting about whether to sell the house where Cassie lives, which might mean moving across town, into another school district, away from all of Cassie's friends and activities. Cassie never knows what mood she'll find her mother in when she comes home from school—sweet and anxious, tired and depressed, or furious and excited about some chore that Cassie has forgotten to do. Lately, Cassie hasn't felt like doing much of anything. She isn't sleeping well, has a hard time waking up in the morning, and just seems to drag her way through the day. She doesn't even have any energy for gymnastics practice, which she used to enjoy. She doesn't feel like being with her friends, and certainly not with her family. All she wants to do is stay in bed.

Malcolm's SATs are coming up soon. Ever since he was in junior high, he and his parents have been planning which college he'll go to. Malcolm's parents don't earn a lot of money, but they're hoping that their straight-A son will do so well on his SATs that he'll get a scholarship to cover all or part of his college costs. Malcolm is excited about the idea of going away to school and proud of himself that he may help pay for part of it. But lately he's been waking up in the middle of the night for "no reason," breathing hard, his heart pounding, as though he's been running. He finds himself worrying about things that never used to bother him, like whether the friend that passed him in the hall without speaking really didn't see him or is actually angry about something Malcolm has done. Often, in the mornings, Malcolm will wake up nervous, as though he's forgotten something important or as though he knows something bad is going to happen, even though he can't find any reason for his fears.

Lou is in love. And he's happier than he's ever been in his life. Marisol, the girl he's been too scared to talk to, has actually asked *him* to a party on Saturday night. She even told him that she's liked him for a long time and was wishing that he'd ask *her* out. What could be better? All day Friday, Lou can't keep his mind on anything else. He doesn't feel like eating lunch and hasn't got much appetite for dinner. His mind keeps wandering, even during basketball practice. Whenever he thinks of Marisol, his heart beats faster, his palms get sweaty, and he has trouble breathing. Lou doesn't think he can stand this much happiness!

What Is Stress?

Lou, Malcolm, and Cassie are all suffering from various kinds of *stress*—demands that life makes on their bodies, their minds, and their feelings. Stress can be caused by many things. Sometimes stress has a physical cause—heat, cold, hunger, or thirst. Sometimes stress is psychological—worry about whether someone likes you, or the unpleasant feelings of a fight with your parents. Stress can come from an event that is happening—as when you're taking a test—or from an event that you are thinking about—as when you're getting ready to take a test. Stress can even come from happy events, such as going out on a hoped-for date, winning a baseball game, or getting into the college of your choice.

As you can see, stress is not a terrible condition to be avoided. It's a normal part of life. And there's no way to avoid it. Even if you managed to live a totally safe, predictable life, one that made absolutely no demands on your mind, your feelings, or your body, you'd probably be bored—which is another kind of stress! Being alive means that life is always making demands on you. Those demands are called *stress.*

Stress Is a Part of Life

The fact that stress can't be avoided may seem like bad news. But actually, it's good news. Once you know that stress is a normal part of life, you can stop wishing for a magic formula that will make all your worries instantly disappear. You can stop envying people who seem to "have it made," those lucky ones who seem to have avoided all the stresses of *your* life. You can recognize instead that the pressures you feel are difficult for everybody—your worries aren't caused by something "wrong with you."

Once you realize that, you may even feel less stressed out already. Now that you're not trying to make stress disappear, you can figure out some ways to cope with it. Maybe you can't expect never to get worried, but you can figure out ways to worry less often. You can look at your worries differently, keeping them in proportion instead of feeling as though they've taken over your life.

Likewise, you may not be able to eliminate all of life's demands. But there are some things you can do to get along more easily with your family, your friends, and your teachers. Right now, these people may seem to be causing you grief; this book can help you figure out some concrete ways to reduce the pressures you may be feeling.

Once you accept that stress is a part of life, you may even discover ways of making stress work for you. This book can also help you turn your worries about a test, a performance, or a game into positive energy that helps you to do better and enjoy the experience more intensely.

Reactions to Stress

The first step to making stress work for you instead of against you is to understand it. What we've been calling "stress" is actually the body's reaction to some demand. You can understand this if you think about the first humans. If they were suddenly caught in a freezing rainstorm or were about to be attacked by a wild beast, their bodies had to respond quickly to these demanding, dangerous conditions. So when humans need to respond to *any* kind of demand, their bodies jump to attention. In fact, your body may respond if you even start *thinking* about a stressful situation—say, if you picture taking a test or imagine going out with your true love on your first date.

You're probably aware of the external symptoms of stress. Most people in demanding situations say that their hearts beat faster, they break out into a sweat or have damp palms, their stomachs clench, their mouths get dry, and they feel a tightness in their chests.

Reactions that you may not be aware of include a rise in blood pressure, your pupils *dilating* (getting wider), and your skin getting flushed. Inside your body, your adrenal glands, thymus, pituitary glands, and lymphatic system are all responding, mobilizing for action.

You might also find that stress leads you to behave a little differently. Some people notice odd or clumsy behavior, such as dropping or spilling things, forgetting things, or pacing around the room, waving their arms. Note that this kind of behavior can result from any type of stress. Being in love or being angry might both result in your heart beating faster, your chest tightening, and your forgetting something you were going to say.

The Three Stages of Stress

According to some scientists, the reaction to a stressful situation can be broken down into three stages. First is the alarm reaction. This is what happens when you first hear bad news (or extremely good news) or when you first sense danger (or feel happiness) coming. Your first reaction may be just to freeze. Some scientists think this is a holdover from animals in the wild, who might avoid danger by freezing, so that an attacker wouldn't be able to see them as easily.

During this first stage, you may feel that you have no resistance; you feel completely vulnerable. All you are aware of is that some new situation is making a demand on you. You may feel completely overwhelmed.

After this first reaction, your resistance sets in. Your body is now ready to adapt to the new demand. In this second stage, your mind and body may become capable of performing far beyond your usual capacity. An athlete who snags an impossibly high fly ball, an actor who improvises brilliantly to cover a piece of scenery collapsing, a student who somehow completes the last 10 test questions in five minutes, a teenager finding a great new way to ask out the attractive person who unexpectedly starts a conversation—all of these people may reach new heights of excellence under the pressure of the moment.

Of course, some people have the opposite reaction. Under the pressure of the stressful situation, they adapt by shutting down or withdrawing. Instead of performing brilliantly, they feel like hiding. Instead of being spurred to new levels of courage, they try to protect themselves by running away. That's why the reaction to stress is often called the "fight or flight reaction"—because you may protect yourself either by fighting back (completing the test, asking for the date) or by running away.

If you once again imagine the early humans living in the wilderness, you can see that both fight and flight were useful reactions. In some situations, such as being faced by a wild animal, the intelligent reaction might indeed be to run away. In other situations, such as being caught in a dangerous storm, there might be nowhere to run to. Then, finding a resourceful way to "fight back" and overcome a situation's difficulties would be necessary to stay alive.

However you adapt to a stressful situation, you inevitably face the third stage of stress—exhaustion. Sooner or later, your ability to resist drops. You feel as though you have come to the end of your resources.

If you're lucky, you won't reach this stage until after the stressful situation has been handled. The athlete who walks off the field or the actor who walks off the stage usually experiences a period of letdown or exhaustion—if not right after the game or the show, then within a few hours. A soldier on the battlefield may experience a similar letdown when the fighting is over. But if the battle goes on for days, the soldier may collapse under the strain while the fighting continues.

Likewise, if you have been studying hard for a special test, you may feel pumped up and excited as you actually take it. Along with your nervousness, you may feel especially sharp and quick. Then, after the test, you may feel let down, tired, or drained.

On the other hand, if you have been studying hard to keep from failing a particularly hard class, your stress may go on for several weeks. Possibly, if you haven't found ways to relax and relieve the stress, you will find yourself "collapsing" at some point—feeling tired and despairing, as though it no longer mattered whether or not you passed your class or as though you no longer had the energy to open another book.

How long you can tolerate stress, and when that third-stage reaction will set in, depends on many factors. A healthy diet, plenty of sleep, and regular exercise are great buffers against the negative effects of stress. They enable you to endure stressful situations for much longer and with much more energy than you would if you were eating poorly and losing sleep. On the other hand, drugs, alcohol, caffeine, and sugar weaken your ability to withstand stress. They deplete your physical and mental resources and actually make it more difficult for you to relax and restore your energy.

As you can see, there is no way to avoid stress completely. But there are many different ways of minimizing stress, and there are also many ways of handling it.

In Chapter 2, we'll look more specifically at stress that becomes *anxiety*—the persistent feeling that something is wrong, or the constant state of being worried. And, in Chapter 3, we'll look at ways to relieve anxiety, both by minimizing stress and by handling it differently. Likewise, in Chapter 4, we'll look at stress that becomes *depression*—a fatiguing loss of energy—with Chapter 5 offering some suggestions for dealing with and relieving depression. Finally, in Chapter 6, we'll talk about ways to get help in handling anxiety and depression, with Chapter 7 offering a concrete list of resources that will actually direct you to help.

First, however, let's look at some of the general causes of stress in your life. Sometimes, just identifying a stressful situation is enough to make it seem less of a pressure.

Teen Stresses

You may have heard your parents or other adults say, "You're young—what do you have to worry about?" From adults, books, or movies, you may have gotten the impression that the teen years are supposed to be a happy, carefree time, that only older people with full-time jobs and family responsibilities are entitled to talk about stress.

Nothing could be further from the truth. The teenage years are some of the most stressful you will ever know. Some of the reasons for this are biological; some are social. In either case, the stresses you face as a teenager are particularly painful precisely because you are young and have not dealt with them before.

One source of teenage stress is simply biology. Your body is changing daily as you go from being a child to being an adult. Girls are developing breasts and getting their periods; boys' voices are changing. Both sexes are going through hormonal changes that produce strong sexual feelings and which can also lead to wild mood swings or powerful emotions.

Some of the stress that goes with these changes is temporary. The rapid changes that your body is undergoing are particular to the teen years. Change is by definition stressful—but once your body has reached adulthood, it won't be changing in the same dramatic way, and some of the stress will automatically be eased.

On the other hand, some of the stress that goes with these changes will be with you for the rest of your life. You'll continue to have sexual feelings and an adult body to which others may respond sexually. Girls will continue to menstruate and possibly to experience emotional reactions to various parts of the menstrual cycle for many years to come. You'll continue to have to make choices about your sexual behavior, about the relationships you want, about how to handle others' responses to you.

As you can see, we've moved from biology into more social issues. All teenagers experience new sexual feelings, but not all societies have the same rules for how to handle them. For example, in some societies, children are married by the age of 13 or committed to marry people chosen by their parents. In other societies, teenagers are strictly chaperoned, kept rigidly apart from members of the opposite sex. In still other societies, teenagers are allowed to experiment sexually with each other, forming short-term relationships that do not lead to marriage. Some societies consider homosexual feelings evil, some don't recognize the existence of them and some are permissive about them.

In our own society, sexual rules and standards are changing rapidly, and it's possible to find a wide variety of standards and beliefs within a single community. You may even find strong disagreements within your own family.

This variety demands that you make a lot more choices than in a more unified society. Even if you and your parents are in complete agreement, you still have to deal with many other standards than the ones held by your family. And if you question your parents' beliefs, you have the added responsibility of making your own choices in an area where few people can agree.

One area that can be stressful for teens is masturbation. Some religions consider this a sinful practice, and some families hold negative attitudes about it. Other people, including many psychologists and doctors, believe that it is a healthy, natural way of finding out more about your body and giving yourself pleasure.

The area of men's and women's roles in dating and relationships is stressful for many people—including most adults! Whereas 30 years ago, dating was regulated by a fairly rigid system of rules—the boy always did the asking, always paid, and was expected to pick the girl up and take her home—now the rules are much more fluid. Now girls can invite boys out on dates, either party can pay or both can share expenses, and a couple may meet somewhere or go out in a group.

Despite the changes, many girls still find themselves uncomfortable with the idea of doing the asking, and many boys are still not sure what's expected of them. A girl may worry that if she asks a boy out, she'll be considered too aggressive or too sexual; a boy may worry that if he *doesn't* do the asking, he's somehow lost ground or hasn't been enough of a man.

Likewise, with sex itself, attitudes have changed—but old attitudes hang on, too. Whereas, once, people assumed that boys were *only* interested in sex and girls were completely *un*interested, now there is more recognition of the fact that both boys and girls are interested in both physical and emotional connections.

At the same time, a girl may worry that having sexual feelings makes her a "slut" or will cause her to lose the respect of others, while a boy may be afraid that if he doesn't score often enough, he isn't a "real man." Or a girl may worry that being less interested in sex than a boy is will cause him to lose interest, while a boy worries that his girlfriend isn't as interested in the physical part of their relationship as he would like her to be. Both girls and boys may be anxious about expressing their sexual feelings, their likes and dislikes, to their partners.

Some teenagers experience particular stress in figuring out their sexuality because they have strong sexual feelings for members of the same sex. In our society, gay people face a great deal of discrimination, so a teenager who thinks that he or she is gay or bisexual (having sexual feelings for people of both sexes) may be especially anxious about his or her sexual feelings.

Teenagers may be worried that their feelings will "make them gay" when they would rather be straight. Or they may accept their own feelings but worry about being ridiculed or abused by others. They may experience particular stress in wanting to approach other teenagers of the same sex, having to wonder not only whether the other person is interested in them but also whether the other person will be receptive to approaches from someone of the same sex.

The stress of dealing with your changing body and your changing feelings can lead to feelings of anxiety or depression. But this period of exploration can also be interesting and exciting. In later chapters, we'll talk more about how to handle these new demands.

Stress and Your Identity

Another pressure of the teenage years has to do with your developing a new adult identity. As you get older, you become more able to question what you have been told and to think for yourself. In our society, especially, the teenage years are marked out as the time when you may want to rethink the ideas that you have taken for granted, about religion, politics, career, life-style, relationships, and just about everything else. Even if, at the end of your thinking, you end up in complete agreement with everything that your family has taught you, it still may feel necessary to think everything through for yourself.

This process brings with it various kinds of stress. For one thing, it may bring you into disagreement with your family or with others in authority. One obvious source of stress that may result is arguments. But, more subtly, you may also feel uncomfortable simply knowing that you and your family do not agree.

Various families allow their members different kinds of leeway to think differently. In some families, children are expected and even encouraged to disagree with parents and think for themselves. In other families, children are expected to be obedient and to recognize that "parents know best." In still other families, children may be told that they have the freedom to think for themselves but receive unspoken messages that it's really not all right to disagree.

These unspoken messages may be the most stressful of all. If you see your parents acting hurt, upset, frightened, or confused when you disagree, you may get the message that you are being a bad person when you think for yourself. It may feel as though simply by thinking independently, you are causing distress to another person. If you can't help thinking independently anyway—and most teenagers can't!—you may feel guilty, angry, or frightened. These feelings may translate into anxiety or depression.

Possibly, you may feel that disagreeing with others will isolate you, so that you are faced with an unpleasant choice between giving in or being all alone. If you see the world in this way, any possible disagreement can be an enormous source of stress, since the stakes for every issue become very high.

There's another reason why developing your own ideas and values may be stressful. When you were a child, you had the security of knowing that your parents were the final authority. You might not have liked or agreed with what they did and thought, but there was a certain safety in knowing that your opinions really didn't matter—your parents were in charge.

Now that you are closer to being an adult, you are beginning to give up that safety. While it is exciting to realize that you can think for yourself, it can also be frightening. Now if you make a mistake, the mistake is yours alone—it's no longer your parents' responsibility to help you straighten it out. Of course, if you achieve something great, the triumph is also yours alone. Either way, making your own decisions and taking responsibility for your own actions is a new demand on you—and so, a new kind of stress.

Some scholars believe that teenagers today have an especially difficult time developing adult identities because the lines between childhood and adulthood have become more blurred. These scholars point out that several decades ago, there were sharp lines between adults, teenagers, and children. These three categories of people dressed differently, had different hairstyles, listened to different types of music, saw different types of entertainment, and had different levels of freedom. Certain "markers" helped define the boundary between childhood and adolescence (the teen years), between adolescence and adulthood, making it clear to everyone which category he or she belonged in.

For example, 30 years ago, most girls did not wear make-up until age 16, or even older. Being allowed to wear make-up meant crossing a real boundary. Now, however, many girls wear make-up at age 13 or younger. Under these circumstances, it's much harder for the 16-year-old girl to measure how close she is to adulthood and how far she is from being a child.

Likewise, 30 years ago, high school students may have planned for college, but basically their responsibilities were limited to completing their high school coursework. Today, high school students are often expected to prepare elaborate applications, to be sure to get into the "right" extracurricular activities, and to take courses to prepare themselves for SATs and PSATs. The level of adult responsibility expected of college-bound teenagers has greatly increased, making it difficult for high school students to understand whether they are teenagers with the freedom to simply live day by day or adults with the responsibility of preparing for a future.

Of course, your abilities and freedoms do change as you move from age 13 to age 16 to age 18 to age 21. But if you tried to name exactly how your status would change with every age change, you might have some difficulty. Dating relationships, drinking, driving, make-up, adult clothes, and late hours used to be restricted to people over the age of 18, or at least 16. Now, many of these things are available by age 13 or even younger, blurring the boundaries.

Likewise, as you move into adolescence, you are likely to experience increased responsibility in school. Instead of remaining in a single classroom, you move from class to class and often have the freedom to choose some of your courses. Instead of simply completing your coursework, you may have your eye on what you want to do after high school, whether your goal is to attend college, to go to vocational school, to get a job, or to take some time off to travel and think. Whatever your choices, the fact is that you have choices to make—and, as we have seen, choices, however positive and exciting, lead to stress.

In the same vein, as you get older you may have increased family responsibilities, such as more household chores or babysitting responsibilities for brothers and sisters. You may also have financial responsibilities, to your family or to yourself, which involve your getting a job or earning money in some other way. These new responsibilities can be exciting ways of finding out who you are and what you can do—but they can also be stressful new demands that take some getting used to.

Family Stresses

In addition to the stresses that come with being a teenager are the stresses that come with being part of a family. Your parents may be going through a divorce or a remarriage. You may have new step-relatives to get used to or you may have to deal with your parents' dating. This can be particularly stressful if you are just beginning to date yourself.

Your parents may also be under stress from their parents, who may be getting older and requiring more help. Perhaps a grandparent or elderly relative is moving in with you, being moved to a nursing home, or just requiring more time and attention from your parents. Or perhaps your brothers or sisters are having children of their own and expecting increased assistance from your parents.

Your parents may be going through their own life changes. They may be concerned with aging, retirement, or their own "mid-life identity crises." They may be grieving over the death of a parent. As you are now a teenager, no longer a child, they may turn to you for increased help or may feel safe in offering you less support. Once again, these changes may feel like tremendous burdens or like exciting new opportunities to try out your new independence. Either way—or both—they will add stress to your life!

Social Stresses

All of us face a certain amount of stress from the society that we live in. Now that you are a teenager, you are more aware than ever of the social problems that affect you and will continue to affect you as you become an adult.

The economy is one major source of stress in U.S. society. Unemployment and inflation bring economic hardship to many people. These issues may be affecting your family directly, or you may simply be living with the unpleasant awareness that many people in your community are homeless, hungry, or unemployed. Since teenage unemployment rates are higher than adult ones, you yourself may be experiencing the frustration of not being able to find a job.

Racism is another source of social stress. Once again, you may feel that this issue affects you directly or is a constant presence in the lives of people you know. You may be concerned about racial incidents or conflicts in your school or your community. You may be aware that racial prejudice affects your own choices about whom you will date or be friends with, about where you will someday live, or work, or go to school.

The threat of war is a very real stress, particularly to teenage boys who will soon be the age at which they must register for the draft. Pollution and the threats to the environment are another type of social stress that may affect you, directly or indirectly.

On a more immediate level, your place in society right now is defined by going to school. The rules of your school—both the spoken rules of the administration and the "unspoken rules" of your fellow students—may be a source of stress to you.

One way or another, these stresses affect everyone in our society. (Adults who don't face the stress of school face similar pressures at their jobs, both from their employers and from their fellow workers.) But they may feel especially frustrating to you for several reasons.

First, you may just be becoming aware of these social stresses. When you were a child, you were probably most concerned with your immediate family and friends. Even if you were aware that racism, unemployment, or pollution was a part of your world, you probably looked to your parents to decide how to handle it. Now that you are becoming more of an adult, you may be taking on these social issues as your own responsibility.

Second, as a teenager, you don't have some of the same resources as an adult to deal with these social stresses. You aren't old enough to vote, and you may find it more difficult to get involved in political groups or community associations working to solve these problems. One big source of stress is feeling powerless and out of control. If you are aware of social problems without imagining how you can help solve them, they will seem doubly stressful to you.

Once again, however, identifying a problem is the first step toward its solution. If you're aware of feeling stress from these social problems, you don't have to feel passive and powerless. You can search for an organization where you can address these problems—or, if one doesn't exist that's right for you, you can start one yourself with other teenagers. At the very least, you can start to study what other people have done to organize for change, to prepare yourself for taking action. One of the best ways to combat stress is to take responsibility for a situation and figure out how *you* want to handle it!

Beyond "Normal" Stress

Throughout this chapter we've emphasized that stress is a part of life. As we'll see in later chapters, some stressful situations can be "solved," while others must simply be endured. But there are some situations that you should not endure. If you are in one of the following stressful situations, you should get help immediately. Tell a sympathetic adult, call a hot line, telephone a social services agency, or call one of the organizations listed in the back of this book. But do *not* remain in any of the following situations without getting help!

- *If someone in your family abuses alcohol or drugs,* particularly a parent or guardian. You may not be able to remove the stress by getting the person to stop his or her abuse—but you can make sure that you are getting the care *you* need. Call Alcoholics Anonymous for suggestions of how to get help, or call Al-Anon (for friends and families of drinkers), Al-A-Teen or Al-A-Tot (for teenagers or children who are friends or relatives of drinkers), Nar-Anon (for friends and families of drug abusers), Nar-A-Teen or Nar-A-Tot (for teenagers or children who are friends or relatives of drug abusers). Numbers for these and other resource groups are in Chapter 7.
- *If someone is sexually abusing you or someone in your family.* Sexual abuse is when an adult or someone in a position of authority is invading your privacy in a sexual way. It can include touching; fondling; inappropriate kissing; watching you or demanding that you watch them while getting undressed, taking a bath, or going to the bathroom; inappropriate tickling or phys-

ical games; or "talking dirty" in a way that makes you uncomfortable; as well as actual sexual intercourse or genital contact. Sexual abuse can come from a family member, a teacher, a religious leader, a family friend, or a stranger; from a man or from a woman. If something makes you uncomfortable, but you aren't sure whether it is sexual abuse, find an adult you can trust and tell him or her about it. Or call an anonymous hot line to talk about your problem (look in the yellow pages or at the list in Chapter 7). Even if the situation has been going on for some time, and you are only now getting the courage to deal with it, find a way to take action by telling someone who can help you. More resources are listed in Chapter 7.

- *If someone is physically abusing you or someone in your family.* Physical abuse can include hitting, beating, being thrown down stairs or against a wall, having things thrown at you, being burned, having your hair pulled, being cut, or receiving any other injury that leaves a scar, requires medical attention, or causes you a great deal of pain. Physical abuse may be presented as "acceptable punishment" in some families, but if the punishment takes one of the forms described above, it is more than punishment, it is abuse, and you deserve to be free of it. Likewise, physical abuse is sometimes excused as the "helpless" actions of a parent who is drunk, on drugs, or "out of control" in some other way. The person who is abusing you may not be a "bad person," but he or she needs help and so do you. Once again, tell a sympathetic adult, call a hot line, or get in touch with one of the resources in Chapter 7.

Coping with Stress

As we have seen, stress is a part of almost every aspect of life. We're used to thinking of "stress" as a bad thing, but it's really only a demand that life makes on our bodies, our minds, and our feelings—a demand that can challenge us to reach new heights of accomplishment, feel more intensely, and get more out of being alive. One way of coping with stress is to see it in this light—as a challenge rather than a problem.

On the other hand, a certain amount of worry, sadness, and frustration is also an inevitable part of life. No matter how good our mental attitudes, life is going to present us with some problems that we can't solve, with some sorrows that we can't rationalize. Learning to cope with life's problems is part of the task of becoming an adult.

In the rest of this book, we'll be talking about what happens when stress becomes overwhelming, when it goes beyond simple worry or sadness and becomes anxiety or depression. And we'll talk about some concrete ways of handling situations so that, even if they remain unpleasant, you can endure them without becoming overly anxious or depressed.

It may help to remember that many of the stresses that you are experiencing now will automatically smooth themselves out as you become older. Family stresses will change radically when you leave home, go away to school, or become self-supporting. The stress associated with dating and relationships will be eased somewhat as you become more experienced in this area, and as you learn to know yourself better. Social stresses may seem more manageable when you have the adult freedom to vote, to join a political group, and to otherwise take action about them.

Meanwhile, everything you learn now about coping with stress will stand you in good stead when you become an adult. The more you learn about yourself and your feelings, the more resources you will have, now and in the future, for enduring life's problems and savoring life's joys.

2

Anxiety

Calvin is a perfectionist. He never likes to turn in school-work unless he's sure it's done exactly right. Although he gets good grades, he worries whenever his score on a test is lower than it was the week before—or when he finds that a classmate has gotten a higher score. Calvin feels extremely uncomfortable about starting any new project or assignment, with the result that he often puts off starting his work until the last minute, even though he may have spent several days "getting ready" to work. With all of his hard work, Calvin is rarely satisfied with anything he does, and if someone pays him a compliment, he's likely to tell that person why he doesn't really deserve it. In fact, getting compliments only seems to make Calvin feel *more* anxious.

Maria is one of the most popular girls at her school. She's editor of the school paper, vice president of the student council, and one of the stars of the gymnastics team. When one of the other girls dropped off the cheerleading squad, the coach asked Maria to fill in. Even though she was already so busy, Maria said yes. Maria also has a steady boyfriend whom she goes out with every weekend, plus a couple of girlfriends that she spends time with after school. No matter how much time she spends with her friends, however, Maria always finds time to keep her grades up. In everyone else's eyes, Maria has it made. And Maria herself thinks that she should be grateful—but why does she always feel like she's failing?

Lisa has always been shy and uncertain. Whenever she meets new people, she worries about what kind of impression she's making. If a boy asks her out on a date, she's so nervous she can barely talk to him, and he rarely asks a second time. Of course, Lisa is too shy to do any asking herself. Sometimes, when she's alone, Lisa starts worrying that she'll never have any real friends or any boyfriends, and she starts to picture how lonely her life will be and how alone she'll be when she gets old and everyone in her family is dead. When she gets these anxious feelings, the one thing that seems to help is eating, so Lisa goes to the kitchen and raids the refrigerator. Right after she's had two helpings of ice cream or a big serving of leftover macaroni and cheese, Lisa does feel calmer—but sooner or later, the worries start again. And now she's also worried about all the weight she's been gaining.

What Is Anxiety?

Calvin, Maria, and Lisa are all suffering from *anxiety.* The dictionary defines anxiety as "a state of being uneasy, apprehensive, or worried about what may happen; concern about a possible future event."

Sometimes anxiety is tied to a *particular* future event—such as when Calvin worries about starting a paper or taking a test. Sometimes anxiety is tied to an *imagined* future event, such as when Lisa pictures herself as old and alone. Sometimes anxiety is experienced as just a *general* state of unease, such as when Maria feels worried for "no good reason."

Although anxiety may be triggered by stress, it's important to understand that anxiety is not necessarily the result of stress. It's possible to feel stress without feeling anxious. An actor or athlete who is nervous and full of stage-fright but also confident and excited about going onstage or onto the field may be experiencing stress, but he or she is not really anxious, just nervous and excited. A student who has a great deal of homework to do may have to take a deep breath and gear up for a weekend full of work—but that student isn't necessarily anxious, just facing a difficult task.

On the other hand, it's possible to feel anxious for no apparent reason, or when something good seems to be happening. In the last chapter, we saw how Malcolm wakes up anxious, worried about something without knowing what. Calvin feels anxious after getting a compliment. Maria feels anxious even when all of her projects and activities are going well.

Because anxiety isn't always easy to explain at first glance, that can make it a frightening feeling to have. It's hard enough to feel worried—but to worry without knowing why may be even harder!

Sometimes people think they know why they're anxious—but on closer examination, their reason isn't really logical. For example, Calvin might say that he's anxious about taking a test. If you pointed out that he's never yet gotten less than an A, so there's no reason to be anxious, he might say, "But there's always a first time," or "But I was just lucky before." Lisa might say that she's worried about what's going to happen in 20 years. If you pointed out that she has no way of knowing what her life will be like in 20 years, she might answer, "But what if I'm right?"

Likewise, a person might be anxious about something out of all proportion to its real importance. Maria, for example, worries so much when one of her friends is mad at her that she can't sleep. She stays up all night, thinking about what a bad person she must be to have this happen to her. Logically, there is a good reason for Maria to be somewhat upset. After all, it's never pleasant to be on bad terms with a friend. But the strength of Maria's feelings seems to go far beyond the incident that is setting them off.

So one of the important things to understand about anxiety is that it is *illogical*. That's our first clue to understanding anxiety. As opposed to nervousness, which relates to a specific event, is more or less in proportion to that event, and goes away when the event is over, anxiety is a state of worry that goes beyond any logical explanation.

The Effects of Anxiety

Ironically, people who are anxious about something bad happening often find that their anxiety actually makes things worse. Calvin's nervousness about taking tests seems to make his brain stop. He has to work three times as hard to remember the answers while he's taking the test as he did when he was only studying. Lisa's nervousness about a date going badly leads to her being unable to talk, laugh, or enjoy herself—and then, of course, her date is almost sure to go badly.

As we saw in the last chapter, anxiety and stress may literally affect your performance. Anxiety can affect your memory, your control and coordination, and your judgment. Under the press of anxiety, you may forget lines on stage or a key play on the basketball court. You may drop things, spill things, or bump into things. You may say something that you regret a minute later, or react too quickly or too slowly to a situation that demands your attention.

Anxiety can also affect your performance indirectly. For example, perfectionists like Calvin experience a great deal of anxiety about doing their work perfectly. Ironically, the result of this anxiety may be that they have a very difficult time getting started. The mere thought of failing worries them so much that they can hardly bear the thought of sitting down to work, so they take advantage of any excuse to procrastinate (put things off).

This procrastination may take the form of finding other things that "just have" to get done, such as washing one's hair or cleaning one's room. It may take the form of preparing "extra well," such as reading far more books than necessary before starting to write a paper, or writing and rewriting an outline over and over. It may take the form of feeling paralyzed, simply sitting and staring at the page or at the pile of books to be studied; wandering off to watch television or get a snack; or scheduling other activities that "just happen" to take up work time.

Procrastination is also a ready-made excuse for *not* doing well. If Calvin ends up writing his paper at three in the morning the night before it's due, no one could possibly expect it to be perfect, could they?

Likewise, the person who over-schedules is giving him- or herself a built-in protection against failure. Maria may be worried about failing, but if she does do badly at one activity, she certainly has a good reason: Look at how many other things she had to do!

In the same way, people who are anxious about failing socially may protect themselves against anxiety by deciding in advance that they know what's going to happen. That way, it isn't really a failure. If Lisa, for example decides that she *knows* her date is going to go badly—or that she knows how awful her life will be in 20 years—the risk of failing may seem easier to bear. She may have "failed" as a date or even as a person, but at least she "succeeded" as a predictor of events!

Even if a person does perform well while anxious, anxiety may sap his or her ability to enjoy an activity. Maria, for example, feels constantly worried about failing. Although she has a loving boyfriend, good friends, and lots of interesting activities, she's unable to take much pleasure in them because she's always worried about the work she *isn't* getting done, the friend she *isn't* keeping happy, the obligation she *isn't* fulfilling. For all his worrying, Calvin does well in school—but he finds it difficult to enjoy either his accomplishments or the work itself. Even when Lisa does get the chance to be with people she likes, she has a hard time relaxing and enjoying their company—she's too worried about what they're thinking of her!

Extreme Anxiety

Most of us experience some kinds of anxiety some of the time. Sometimes we can turn our anxiety into relaxation—or into pleasurable anticipation of a new challenge. Sometimes we simply have to endure our anxiety and try to keep it in perspective. Either way, anxiety isn't really dangerous, it's just unpleasant.

Sometimes, however, anxiety becomes more severe. In those cases, it can cause serious problems to our health or our ability to function.

Anxiety-Related Illness

Many illnesses can actually be understood as our bodies' response to anxiety. Prolonged feelings of anxiety can lower our general resistance to illness. Anxiety can also set off headaches, indigestion, neck and back pain, and fatigue. In more serious cases, it can produce ulcers, colitis (a disease of the colon, one of the digestive organs), high blood pressure, heart and circulation problems, and severe back problems. In many cases, asthma, a disease that involves difficulty breathing, is related to anxiety as well, with intense anxiety setting off asthma attacks, or periods of difficulty breathing.

Anxiety Attacks

Sometimes people feel so anxious they have what are known as *anxiety attacks.* They may feel their hearts pounding, their heads throbbing, or their pulses racing. They may have difficulty breathing, feeling as though their chest and lungs are tightening up and suffocating them—or they may be panting, breathing hard, as though they've been running. They may feel in the grip of fear or they may feel numb, as though they're beyond feeling. An anxiety attack can make a person feel dizzy, nauseous, faint, or simply weak.

Medically, these "attacks" are caused by emotional reactions, rather than by any physical factor. Although they may feel life-threatening, they are really no more dangerous than a headache or an upset stomach. However, prolonged anxiety or repeated severe anxiety attacks are definitely bad for your health. If you find that you are being incapacitated by anxiety attacks, it may be a sign that you should seek counseling or some other kind of professional help in dealing with your emotions (see Chapters 6 and 7). At any rate, you may want to look at some of the relaxation techniques described in the next chapter.

Compulsive Behavior

Some people try to keep anxiety at bay by certain kinds of repeated behavior or rituals. They may have certain routines to help them cope with situations that make them anxious, like tapping out each floor number in an elevator or washing their hands after an unpleasant situation.

To some extent, routines and rituals can be useful ways of coping with anxiety. If studying makes you anxious, for example, it might be soothing to have a regular routine of sharpening your pencils, cleaning your desk, and pouring yourself a big glass of milk as you sit down to work. Before a date it might be calming to have a ritual of taking a long, hot bath, listening to a special piece of music or repeating an encouraging phrase to yourself.

Sometimes, though, a person's routines or rituals may become more elaborate and demanding than the ordinary life events that they are meant to help cope with. And if a routine is unavoidably broken, a person may feel even more anxious than before. If, for example, an athlete refuses to start the game without her lucky t-shirt, she isn't coping with her anxiety, she's being ruled by it. Likewise, if someone's hand-washing "ritual" takes 15 minutes and is overly elaborate (always the left hand first, then the right, one finger at a time, always in the same order), it has probably gone beyond being a simple coping mechanism and become *compulsive behavior*—behavior that a person feels *compelled*, or forced, to do.

If you find yourself engaging in compulsive behavior that is disrupting your life, such as elaborate rituals that take inordinate amounts of time, you may need help in learning to cope with your anxiety in other ways. See Chapters 6 and 7 for more information on the types of help that are available.

Eating Disorders

Some people cope with anxiety through their relationship to food. To some extent, it's not a serious problem if a person is occasionally too nervous to eat, or if he or she sometimes turns to a candy bar or a favorite food in the middle of an anxious time.

Sometimes, however, eating patterns triggered by anxiety (and other feelings) can get out of control and become *eating disorders*—a relationship to food that seriously disrupts a person's life and threatens his or her health.

The most common eating disorders are *anorexia* (refusing to eat, self-starvation), *bingeing* (eating huge amounts of food at one time), and *bulimia* (bingeing and then purging through vomiting or laxatives). All of these can be dangerous to your health—and all are clues that some buried feelings are not being dealt with. Likewise, *compulsive eating* (feeling compelled, or forced, to eat in certain situations; feeling out of control and unable to stop oneself from eating) may be a response to anxiety. As we saw with Lisa, sometimes it seems that only food will calm a person down—but that solution is always temporary. Sooner or later, if it has not been dealt with, the anxiety will return.

If you or someone you know is suffering from an eating disorder, get help immediately. Call one of the hot lines or organization numbers listed in Chapter 7, telephone a local social service agency or clinic, or talk to a counselor who understands about eating disorders.

Drug and Alcohol Abuse

Many people turn to drugs or alcohol as a way of coping with anxiety. Unfortunately, this may create more problems than it solves.

Both drugs and alcohol sap the body of resources that it needs to handle stress. Regular use of either substance puts a tremendous strain on the liver, the organ that washes toxins (poisons) out of the blood. (The nicotine in cigarettes and the caffeine in coffee, tea, cola, and chocolate puts a similar stress on the liver.)

In addition, an excessive use of drugs or alcohol can lead to addiction, which creates anxieties of its own. Along with the original problems that caused anxiety, the addicted person now has the new problem of getting enough alcohol or drugs to satisfy the addiction. In some cases, it may seem easier to worry about getting drugs or alcohol than to be frightened of not having friends, failing in school, or disappointing one's parents. Or it may seem as though the drugs or liquor actually do relieve anxiety for a time. Eventually, however, the original worries come back, just as they do for the compulsive eater.

Ironically, many doctors once recommended diazepam (known by the trade name Valium) or other tranquilizers to help people cope with their anxieties. While it was less usual to prescribe such medication to teenagers, many teens saw their parents turning to medication to cope with their anxieties.

Now we understand that diazepan and most other tranquilizers are addictive and that the medical consequences of taking them regularly are quite severe. Some doctors do continue to prescribe such medication, but most agree that it's better to work out anxieties in other ways.

If you or someone you know has turned to liquor or drugs as a way of coping with anxiety, we urge you, too, to call one of the hot lines or organizations listed in Chapter 7. You deserve a solution that will really help you to cope with your anxieties, not a temporary fix that will only create more problems.

Self-Destructive Behavior

In some extreme cases, a person's anxiety may become so great that it seems easier to hurt oneself, or even to die, than to find a way to deal with the overwhelming feelings of worry. Such self-destructive behavior might take the form of reckless driving or other reckless actions, causing oneself pain, or actually planning to commit suicide.

If you or someone you know is engaging in self-destructive behavior, we urge you to get help immediately. Talk to a sympathetic adult you can trust, call a confidential hot line, telephone a social service agency, or find a counselor. More information about coping with self-destructive behavior and suicidal feelings can be found in Chapter 5, and specific numbers and organizations to call can be found in Chapter 7.

Where Does Anxiety Come From?

So far, we've been focusing on what anxiety feels like and what its effects are. But where does anxiety come from? If it isn't actually *caused* by the things that set it off, what does cause it?

Anxiety is a complicated emotion, and there are many possible factors that might cause it. But one simple rule of thumb is that anxiety comes from *buried feelings.*

These buried feelings might include anger, guilt, sadness, or fear. Any feeling that is too painful to admit and has been buried might show itself again as anxiety.

How does this work? As we are growing up, we have many feelings that are painful and difficult. Sometimes these feelings seem too painful for us to bear. Other times, we worry that these feelings may mean that we are "bad people." In either case, we may handle these difficult feelings by burying them—trying to stuff them down and pretend that we don't have them.

For example, Maria has been brought up to believe that a good girl should always try to make other people happy. Sometimes, though, she just doesn't care what other people want. Sometimes, she would just like to please herself. In fact, sometimes she actually gets angry with all the people who seem to expect so much from her.

Because of what she has been taught, Maria doesn't like these feelings of hers. She thinks that wanting to please herself rather than others is a bad thing, and having that feeling makes her feel guilty and ashamed. And she feels even more guilty about feeling angry. So she tries to make these feelings go away.

But feelings are stubborn. If you try to hide them or pretend them away, they will always come back. So Maria's anger at other people for making demands on her comes back as anxiety and the worry that she is always failing. If Maria could admit that sometimes she doesn't feel like doing what other people want and that sometimes she gets angry, she might not feel so anxious.

In Calvin's case, the feeling that he is trying to hide is sadness. Calvin's father left the family when Calvin was only five. Calvin's mother has always depended on Calvin a great deal. Sometimes he even feels like he's supposed to be *her* parent, instead of the other way around.

Calvin was only a child when his father left, and even now he is only a teenager. He isn't ready to take care of someone else—he still needs someone to take care of *him.* Deep down, Calvin feels very sad that his father left, and he feels sad that his mother can't always give him the support he needs. But these are very painful feelings. It isn't easy for a child to be aware that his or her parents can't give the love and support that is needed. So Calvin tries to make himself believe that he doesn't feel sad, he doesn't need anything, and there is no problem.

Calvin's sad feelings won't just go away, however. They come back as anxiety. Instead of feeling sad and frightened and perhaps angry that his parents can't take care of him as he would like, Calvin worries that he can't take care of himself. He acts as though performing perfectly on his schoolwork would mean that he is strong enough to handle any situation. Instead of expecting more from his parents, which he knows he won't happen, Calvin expects more from himself—and then feels anxious when he can't perform as well as he would like.

Lisa also feels sad and angry about her family situation, but in her case, she finds it difficult even to say what's wrong. Her parents appear to be happily married, and for all appearances, they love Lisa very much. The family has enough money, and Lisa would seem to have every advantage.

Beneath the surface, however, Lisa senses that something is very wrong. When she goes to hug her mother, her mother might hold Lisa off at arm's length and say, "Don't you look pretty today!" On the surface, Lisa's mother is giving Lisa a compliment, but underneath, Lisa is being given the message that her mother doesn't want to hug her.

Because this is a very unpleasant message, Lisa would rather not believe that it was true—it makes her feel too sad. Besides, her mother is always saying how much she loves Lisa, so it makes Lisa feel guilty to disagree and to go on her own instincts that her mother actually isn't being very loving. It also makes Lisa angry that her mother doesn't love her anymore—but once again, she can't admit to herself either that she believes that her mother doesn't love her or that she is angry about it.

Lisa has to do something with all the thoughts and feelings that she is trying not to have. She thinks she has buried them—but they are really coming out in her anxiety. Instead of feeling sad and angry that she isn't being loved enough now, Lisa feels anxious that she might not be loved enough in the future.

Attitudes That Feed Anxiety

So far, we've seen that anxiety can come from buried feelings. In addition, anxiety can come from certain attitudes. Take a look at the following list. How many of these attitudes do you recognize? How many do you hold yourself?

1. People are more likely to remember your one mistake than the 20 good things you did.
2. If you are a nice enough person, no one will ever be mad at you or disappointed in you.
3. Only selfish people put themselves first; unselfish people are always more concerned with other people than with themselves.
4. A really good friend is someone who never lets you down or disappoints you in any way.
5. If somebody really loves you, they won't do anything to hurt you.
6. A person who doesn't meet his or her goals is irresponsible and untrustworthy.
7. You should always finish what you start.
8. It's more important to look at your mistakes and short-comings than to look at your strengths and successes—otherwise, how will you ever learn?

9. I'm an "all or nothing" person—if I can't have everything I want, the one thing I don't have will bother me more than the many things I do have.
10. The one person who doesn't speak to me at a party means more to me than the five people who are happy to see me.
11. As soon as I accomplish something, I like to forget about it and go on to the next thing; I don't want to rest on past successes.
12. I often think about my past mistakes and try to figure out how I could have done things differently.

Sound familiar? These attitudes contribute to anxiety by helping you to focus on what's wrong with your life instead of what's right with it and by encouraging you to hold unrealistic expectations of yourself and other people. Here's how:

Focusing on the Bad Instead of the Good

Statements 1, 8, 9, and 10 all reflect the attitude that since your mistakes outweigh your strengths, you cannot rest until you have eliminated all of your mistakes. Since such perfection isn't possible, this attitude practically guarantees anxiety.

With this attitude, whenever you make a mistake, no matter how small, you may feel overwhelmed by it. Since the mistake counts so much more than the good things you have done, you have no way to put your mistake in perspective, to evaluate realistically how to deal with it and how serious it is. Instead, you may simply feel anxious and upset.

Furthermore, this attitude suggests that your mistakes somehow creep into your strengths and successes, making them less worthwhile. One psychologist says that this is like seeing mistakes as food coloring. Even a tiny drop or two can color an entire quart of water. Likewise, this attitude suggests that even a tiny mistake or two can color an entire day or year of successes. Thus, the one person at a party with whom you were not successful seems to invalidate all the people who are interested in you. Somehow, they don't count, while the disinterested person's judgment seems more accurate.

Focusing on the Past and Worrying About the Future

Statements 11 and 12 both come from the attitude that it's somehow wrong to enjoy and take pride in what you are doing. Instead, your attention is directed to past mistakes and future challenges.

Sometimes it *is* important to think back on the past and to try to learn from it. And it's often helpful to look forward to the future, making plans and gearing up for new challenges. But if that's keeping you from enjoying the present, then you may be holding attitudes that are creating anxiety for you. After all, you can't change the past, and you can't do anything about the future until it happens. Too great a focus on either can make you feel anxious and out of control—while minimizing the good things in your life.

Expecting Others or Yourself to Be Perfect

Expecting perfection is a tricky business. We have all sorts of ways of doing so without really admitting it. "I don't expect my boyfriend to be perfect," someone might say. "But I don't think he should *ever* hurt my feelings."

Or a person might say, "I know nobody's perfect, but only a really *bad* son would forget his father's birthday the way I did."

Of course, sometimes other people do treat us badly, and it's important to recognize when that happens. And if you feel that you are continually letting others down, you might want to ask yourself what's going on—are you angry with somebody? Have you taken on too many commitments? Did you get drawn into promising something that you didn't want to do in the first place?

But expecting perfection from others or yourself is another kind of trap. Statements 4, 5, 6 and 7 are all about holding impossible ideals that no one could ever meet. Expecting that a good friend will never let you down or that a boyfriend or girlfriend will never hurt your feelings is like saying that you and that other person really aren't separate people. It's as though you expected another person to read your mind and feel your feelings, instead of having thoughts, feelings, and wishes of his or her own. If this is your attitude, then it will naturally make you anxious when you come up against the reality that this other person is in fact a separate person.

Likewise, expecting yourself always to finish what you start and always to meet every goal is setting yourself up for disappointment—and, perhaps, anxiety. Sometimes people fail. You can be committed to pursuing excellence while still accepting the reality that you will not always reach it. *Not* accepting that reality is likely to make you feel very anxious, since you will always be worrying about whether you can achieve something that is in fact impossible.

Focusing on Others at Your Own Expense

Statements 2 and 3 are also based on an unrealistic attitude that is likely to produce anxiety whenever reality intervenes. Statement 2 is based on a fantasy about being able to control other people—the idea that, if only *you* are nice enough, other people will have to do what you want.

In fact, no matter how nice or good you are, it's possible that some other people will decide to be angry with you or to dislike you, for reasons of their own. Maybe you remind them of someone else they don't like. Maybe they have always hated people with blond hair or brown eyes.

Maybe they are just jealous of how nice you are! For whatever reason, it's possible that, throughout your life, some people will be angry with you or dislike you. Expecting that you can prevent this is likely to make you feel anxious whenever you discover the truth—that other people's feelings are simply out of your control.

Both statements 2 and 3 suggest that what other people think is very important. This focus on others is likely to create anxiety, since, when all is said and done, there's really nothing you can do about what other people think or how they act.

Likewise, if you expect yourself always to put others first, you will naturally feel anxious—because no one can *always* put other people first. Always putting other people first isn't even a good thing. If you don't take care of yourself, who else will take care of you?

Often people who put others first are secretly hoping that those others will respond by putting *them* first. Isn't it simpler just to take care of yourself and to let other people do the same?

Of course, sometimes, it's important to make sacrifices and to put other people first. Even in those situations, however, there's nothing wrong with feeling that you'd *rather* put yourself first, no matter how you actually act. Not being able to accept these feelings—feeling guilty about them or considering them "selfish"—may lead you to try to bury them, which may in turn lead to anxiety.

How Others May Feed Your Anxiety

Sometimes the messages we get from other people help trigger feelings of anxiety or help support the attitudes we just discussed. If your parents, for example, are much more concerned with the "C" you got in biology than with the "A" you got in math, you may easily get the message that a mistake counts far more than a success. If your employer docks you for being five minutes late and threatens to fire you if it ever happens again, you may easily feel that you can't afford to make even one small mistake. If your boyfriend or girlfriend expects you never to let him or her down, or if your best friend is furious and hurt whenever the two of you disagree, you may well feel justified in thinking that only bad people hurt the ones they love.

These messages can be powerful indeed, especially when they are coming from your family. After all, you've been living in your family—or in some family-like place— since you were a very small child. The very first things you learned about the world, you learned from the adults who took care of you. That makes it difficult to disagree with those adults now. Even if you *say* you disagree with your parents, you may have the deep-down nagging feeling that maybe they are right.

Maria, for example, would like to have a more relaxed attitude about her friends and relationships. But she notices that if her boyfriend calls when Maria is out, her mother is very anxious until Maria calls him back. If Maria says, "I'm busy now, I'll call him back tonight," Maria's mother says, "You better call him now, or else he might get tired of waiting for you." Even though Maria tells her mother not to be so silly, deep down she wonders whether maybe her mother might be right. She doesn't call—but she does feel anxious.

Likewise, when Lisa is getting ready to go out on a date, her father may tell her that she isn't dressed up enough. Lisa might argue and insist that her clothes are fine and he just doesn't understand the latest fashions. She might even win the argument. But deep down, she can't help wondering whether her father knows something she doesn't. After all, he's an adult and a man. Maybe she really isn't looking as good as she had hoped. Lisa may push these feelings away and continue to dress in the way she prefers—but she may also feel anxious.

Coping with Anxiety

As we have seen, there are many sources of anxiety: your own buried feelings, your attitudes and expectations, the messages you get from others. In fact, it may seem like anxiety itself is an overwhelming problem from which there is no escape!

The bad news is that a certain amount of anxiety and worry are probably unavoidable. Very few people are able to avoid anxiety and worrying altogether.

The good news, though, is that there are many ways of coping with anxiety. Sometimes you can eliminate it altogether; sometimes the best you can do is to put it into perspective. Either way, learning more about your feelings and becoming more of an adult means that you are gaining many new resources for coping with anxiety. These resources may not have been available to you when you were a child, but they are available to you now. In the next chapter, we'll take a closer look at some of the ways that you can learn to cope with your anxiety.

3

Coping with Anxiety

The first step to relieving your anxiety is understanding it. In Chapter 2, we looked at some of the thoughts and feelings that might feed anxiety. In this chapter, we'll help you become more aware of *your* patterns of anxiety—what sets them off, how they work, how they affect you. Then we'll go on to make some suggestions for relieving and coping with anxiety.

In this chapter, you will find a variety of suggestions for coping with anxiety. Some ideas focus on your mind, others on your body, still others on your environment or on your interpersonal skills. You may find all of the suggestions helpful, or only some of them. Let your own instincts be your guide. Leaf through the chapter, taking what works for you and leaving the rest alone. We urge you to keep an open mind, however. If an idea catches your fancy, give it a chance! You won't lose anything if it doesn't work—and you might learn a whole new way of coping!

What Makes Me Anxious?: A Checklist

Take a look at the following checklist. On a separate piece of paper, rate each item from 1 to 4, along the following scale:

1—Doesn't bother me at all
2—Bothers me once in a while
3—Makes me somewhat anxious
4—Makes me very anxious

Don't think about these answers too much. Just read through the list and put down the first thing that comes into your mind.

I am anxious about . . .

__ Talking to my parents or guardians
__ Talking to my brothers or sisters
__ Talking to teachers
__ Talking to classmates
__ My relationship with my boyfriend or girlfriend
__ My relationship with a friend
__ Talking to people I don't know
__ Speaking or performing in public
__ Doing homework
__ Being graded
__ Getting into college
__ Getting the job I want
__ Getting married
__ Having children
__ The future in general
__ Fears of not having enough money
__ Fears of not having the right clothes

__ Fears about how I look—my weight, skin, general appearance

__ Going out on a date

__ Asking someone for a date

__ Being asked for a date

__ The idea of having a physical or romantic relationship

__ The idea of not having a physical or romantic relationship

__ Fears that someone is angry with me

__ Guilt that I am angry with someone else

__ Feeling that I am disappointing my parents

__ Relations with my parents' new partners

__ Relations with step-brothers or step-sisters

__ What else? Quickly, without thinking about it, write down anything else that is making you anxious, in list form. Then look at your list and rate it 1, 2, 3, or 4.

Now look back at your list and your ratings. On a separate sheet of paper, copy down anything that makes you anxious that you rated 4. Skip a line and copy down everything that you rated 3, then skip a line again and copy down the 2s.

"Dream It—and Do It!"

Now that you've identified some things that are making you anxious, you can begin to cope with the anxiety. Following is an exercise in *visualization*, or picturing things in your mind. Visualization helps you to imagine new possibilities for yourself. It allows you to draw on the hidden powers of your mind and your imagination to get in touch with parts of yourself that you might be hiding.

First, use visualization to clarify exactly what is making you anxious. On a third sheet of paper, write down one item from your 4 list. Take a deep breath and try to visualize, or picture, the situation that you're referring to. Use as much detail as possible. If you're thinking about taking a test, see yourself in the classroom, holding a pen, getting ready to write. If you're concerned about a relationship, picture everything you can about the person.

Now start to use all five senses to make the picture as real as possible. *See* yourself sitting next to the person you're thinking of. *Smell* the person's shampoo, perfume, or shaving lotion; *hear* the person's voice. Or, if you're taking a test, *feel* the pen in your hand—is it smooth or rough, large or small? *Hear* the sound of the pen scratching on paper; *see* the color of the ink.

As you visualize the anxious situation, allow yourself to feel whatever it is that makes you anxious. Then write it down.

What you write down doesn't have to make sense to anybody else. You might find yourself writing just a single word, such as *angry,* or *stupid.* You might find yourself writing a clear sentence of explanation, like "I'm afraid I'll fail and my parents will be mad," or "I think Terry thinks I'm stupid." Or you might find yourself writing a paragraph or even a page or two, going on about your feelings and thoughts. Some people find it helpful to draw a picture, a design, or a doodle that expresses their feelings.

Whatever you do, it helps to be as specific as possible. If the situation makes you feel "bad," name what that bad feeling is. If you feel frightened about something, write down exactly what is frightening you. Again, don't worry about your words making sense to anyone else. Keep going until you feel that you have expressed your feelings to yourself.

Now go back to visualizing the situation again. This time, imagine the situation working out in a way that no longer makes you feel anxious. Instead, you feel happy, excited, peaceful, or interested. If you are picturing taking a test, for example, you might visualize yourself becoming excited about getting one right answer after another. If you are worried about a relationship, you might imagine the person telling you exactly what you want to hear—or you might imagine yourself behaving in the best possible way you can imagine anyone behaving.

Once again, be as specific as possible. If you are picturing the test, see the questions and see yourself writing the correct answers. See the color of the ink and feel the texture of the paper. Feel your heart beating with the excitement of knowing everything you want to know. Breathe deeply with the satisfaction of checking off one answer after another.

If you are picturing a relationship, hear yourself saying just what you would like to say to the other person. See the color of the person's eyes and notice how his or her eyes look as you say or do what you would like. Hear your voice saying what you imagine, and then hear the other person's voice answering you.

If you find in this exercise that you are slipping back into picturing an anxious or unhappy situation, stop, take a deep breath, and start again. You may be so used to imagining bad things that it takes some effort on your part to imagine something good. With practice, however, you will be able to visualize yourself as free of anxiety, as capable, powerful, and behaving in a way that makes you feel proud.

When you have finished visualizing the new situation, go back to that third sheet of paper, the one where you wrote about the thing that was making you anxious. Below what you wrote, or on the other side of the page, write your feelings about the good situation you imagined. Then write how you acted and what you did to make the situation turn out well. Once again, you may find yourself writing anything from a single word to several pages—or you may find yourself drawing or doodling to express yourself visually. Possibly, doing this exercise will set off other thoughts and feelings that will move you to write or draw further.

When you have finished, do one final thing. Take another deep breath and concentrate for a moment on the good situation that you pictured. Then write or draw yourself a message that you can take with you the next time you encounter the situation that first made you anxious. You might want to recall one image that you imagined, such as the sight of the pen on paper, or the sound of your voice as you said something wonderful. You might want to remember a "lesson" or a "moral," such as "Stay calm," "I am smart," or "I know what to say." You might want to carry the image of the design you drew or a sentence that you wrote. Whatever you choose, write or draw it in a different colored ink at the bottom of the page.

Then, next time you are in an anxious situation, recall your message to yourself. See in your mind how your message looks at the bottom of the page. Remember the color of the ink, feel the pen in your hand as you wrote or drew your message, smell the odors of the room where you were writing, hear the sounds you heard then. Allow this memory to remind you of the way you pictured the good situation. How did you act in that situation? How did you feel? Allow the memory to help you to feel and act that way in real life.

Different people respond to this exercise differently. Some people find that it helps them handle an anxious situation without fear, discovering in themselves new resources and capabilities that they never before suspected. Other people find that while they are still anxious, the exercise helps them to make different, more satisfying choices in the anxious situation, acting more freely and more powerfully. You may find that this exercise helps you right away or that it takes some practice and some ups and downs before you are satisfied. Either way, however, this exercise will help you discover some new options for anxious situations and some new abilities within yourself.

Affirmations: Thinking Positively

Many people find it helpful to calm themselves by using *affirmations*—statements that *affirm*, or reinforce, something good or positive about yourself. The following is a list of examples of affirmations.

I am beautiful (or handsome).
I am loved.
I deserve all the love I want.
I am smart.
I am successful.
I work hard and I achieve great things.
I can do anything that I decide to do.
My friends love me and care for me.
I am a good and loving person.
I bring joy into the lives of those I love.

You may use affirmations from the list, or you can write your own. Just be sure that your affirmations are all expressed in a positive, definite way. No "I mights" or "I shoulds"—and no "don'ts," "nos" or "nots"!

Notice, too, how affirmations are all focused on the present, rather than on the future or the past. If you wanted to write an affirmation about getting good grades, for example, it would not be helpful to write "I will get an A next month" or "I got an A last semester." Instead, you might write, "I am getting the grades I want," or "I am doing excellent work in class."

People use their affirmations in different ways. Most people find it useful to repeat one or two affirmations several times when they get up each morning and before they go to bed each night. Or you might incorporate your affirmations into some other daily routine, such as making your bed, washing the dishes, taking a shower, or brushing your teeth.

Some people tape their affirmations to their mirrors or put them in their notebooks—anywhere they are likely to see them often and be moved to repeat them once or twice. Something about making these affirmations a regular part of your routine seems to help free up new parts of yourself.

Many people find these affirmations helpful at particularly anxious times. People with eating disorders, for example, might say, "I am beautiful," or "I love my body" at times when they feel especially anxious and compelled to turn to food or to self-starvation to relieve their anxiety. They replace their bingeing, purging, or ritual of not eating with an affirmation, calming themselves in a new way.

Other people find affirmations helpful before speaking in public, taking a test, going out on a date, attending a party, or confronting a person with whom they are having difficulties. You can use the information from the previous exercise to help you decide when affirmations might be helpful to you.

You may be wondering why affirmations work, especially if they don't seem true to you right now. For example, if you are anxious about your appearance, it may seem silly or even upsetting to repeat the affirmation "I am beautiful." You may be thinking, "That's fine for people who *are* beautiful, but the whole problem is, I'm not!"

In fact, the reason that affirmations do work is because our minds have so much power over our experience and our lives. Many people seem beautiful, not because they have features that look a certain way, but because they have a kind of self-confidence that encourages others to think that they are beautiful. If you think of some of the most popular girls or boys you know, and think about how they look, you'll probably find that while some may be especially pretty or handsome, others have looks that aren't really all that special. Nevertheless, some other quality makes them attractive. If you feel beautiful or handsome in that way, you too can gain that special self-confidence that helps attract others.

Likewise, focusing on what's positive helps to reinforce it. You may feel that in reality, sometimes you are smart and sometimes you are dumb. Your affirmation, however, will only focus on being smart—not because that's the only reality, but because that's the piece of reality you want to build up and strengthen.

Sports trainers have found that if athletes continually praise themselves and give themselves positive reinforcement, their games automatically improve. When a basketball player makes a shot, for example, she might say to herself, "I made that shot! Good for me! I was accurate, and my timing was perfect." If she misses the shot, she might say, "I was really making a great effort! I had a lot of power behind the ball. My footwork was good, too." Even though she missed the shot, she's not focusing on what she did wrong, but on what she did right. Interestingly, this focus on the positive seems to be more helpful than being "accurate," since it actually does improve games!

If you are interested but skeptical, why not make the experiment? For two whole weeks, try to avoid giving yourself negative criticism. No matter what happens, think positively. Find something to compliment yourself about in every situation. Pick two or three affirmations or write your own and say them to yourself every morning, every night, and every time you feel anxious. At the end of two weeks, take a look at your life. Have things improved? Are you feeling more positive and less anxious? If so, keep experimenting with ways to make affirmations and positive thinking work for you.

Relaxation Exercises

So far, we've been concentrating on ways to reduce anxiety that focus on your mind. Now let's look at some exercises that focus on your body.

These relaxation exercises can be used in two ways. You can do them in your room at home, with the goal of achieving a total state of relaxation. You may find them useful as a regular routine or for times when you are feeling especially stressed-out and anxious.

Once you have mastered these simple techniques, you may find that they are useful in the middle of anxiety-provoking situations as well. Breathing techniques in particular can be used in the middle of a hectic day, before or during a test, in a quick "bathroom break" from a difficult situation, or on your way to or from school. Both the technique itself and the simple fact of "taking a break" from your anxiety will help to calm you down!

Breathing Exercises

A major key to relaxation is breathing. People who meditate focus on achieving heightened mental states through breathing techniques (for more on meditation, see the section just after this one). Actors and singers also use breathing to calm themselves before and during anxious moments on stage.

Many people aren't even aware of what it feels like to breathe deeply. To gain this awareness, lie down on the floor, flat on your back. (You may lie down on your bed, but your concentration won't be as good—and you might fall asleep!)

Allow your back to sink into the floor. If you're more comfortable this way, raise your knees so that your feet are flat against the floor. Now place your hands on your stomach and breathe deeply.

Do you feel how your lungs fill with air and your stomach seems to expand? That's deep breathing. In deep breathing, the breath comes not from the nose, mouth, throat, or chest but from the diaphragm, deep down in the region around your stomach.

Continue breathing deeply, in and out, as you pay attention to everything that you can about how it feels. Don't push your breath, but let it fall in and float out easily and naturally. You might want to sigh gently or make a low noise as you let your breath out. It may be helpful to consciously slow your breathing down, breathing in on a count of four, out on a count of four, then in on a count of five, out on five, and so on, for as many counts as you can manage without straining.

Once you are sure you know what it feels like to breathe deeply, get up—slowly, so as not to disturb the relaxation you may already be feeling. Place your hands on your stomach once more and duplicate the deep breathing you just completed on the floor. If necessary, use a count to slow yourself down, until you are breathing in on no less than a slow count of 10 and breathing out to the same count.

As you've probably discovered by now, this exercise alone is relaxing. What's more, you can practice your deep breathing without being noticed, any time, any place. Some people find it helpful to breathe in on a count of one, out on one, in on two, out on two, and so on, up to 10 or 12, as a way of helping themselves slow down. You might practice this deep breathing before, during, or after an anxious time, or every morning and every night as an overall relaxer.

Muscle Relaxation

Using your deep breathing, you may now add another component of relaxation, focusing on your muscles. Be sure to continue your regular, slow, deep breathing throughout this exercise. If you find yourself tightening up, stop and go back to deep breathing once again until you are breathing slowly and deeply.

By the way, it might help you to make a tape of this exercise or to allow someone you trust to read it to you. Some people find it easier to learn this exercise if there is a voice for them to follow while they are doing it.

Once again, lie flat on your back. Although you may later want to do this exercise lying on your bed or on a couch, you might try it the first time on the floor, so that your concentration will be highest.

Find a comfortable position. Keep your legs stretched out, but let them roll a little apart if you like. Leave your arms lying down at your sides or sticking straight out, but keep them flat on the floor. Let your hands rest loosely on the floor—don't press or force them into any particular position. Find a comfortable position for your head, but be sure you are looking up at the ceiling, not forward at your feet. When you have settled into a position that works for you, close your eyes.

Start with your toes and work up through the soles of your feet, your ankles, calves, thighs, buttocks, lower back, upper back, shoulders, elbows, forearms, wrists, fingers, neck, scalp, and face. Feel each part of your body, one at a time. Notice whatever tension is there and allow it to seep away. Sometimes a tense muscle gets tight before it loosens up. Allow this to happen. You might want to tighten up a muscle yourself, then allow it to relax.

You may find it helpful to visualize the tension in each muscle. You may want to picture a particular color that changes as the muscle relaxes, say, from red (tense) to green or blue (relaxed). Or you may prefer to picture relaxation creeping up from muscle to muscle, like a warm bath or a strong ray of sunlight. You may picture the tension running out of your muscles like dirty water, leaving your muscles clean and dry. Use whatever image works for you.

When you have worked all the way from your toes up through your face and scalp, lie for a moment being aware of your body as a whole. (Remember to keep breathing!) If you are aware of any new or remaining tension, go to that muscle and ask it to relax. Stay focused until you have relaxed completely. Then, very slowly, sit up, then stand. Take a moment to remember this feeling of relaxation.

You may find it helpful to recall this relaxed feeling the next time you are in an anxious situation. It may also help to identify which muscles are tense and then to focus on relaxing them, using your breathing to help you. Some people find it helpful to breathe in while tensing up a muscle and then to slowly breathe out while relaxing it. Learning about which muscles tense up when you are anxious, and then learning how to relax them, is one very helpful way of relieving anxiety.

Meditation

There are many different meditation techniques. If meditation appeals to you, you might go to a local bookstore, yoga center, health-food store, or Eastern Studies department of a local college to try to find classes or teachers who can help you learn more about it. Here we include only a simplified version of this rich and fascinating discipline, to give you a taste of what it might hold for you.

Meditation is a way of clearing the mind and allowing you to free yourself of anxiety and worries. It is most effective if you meditate for about 20 minutes each morning and each evening, but you may wish to start at about 10 minutes and work up. Some people prefer to meditate only once a day or only at stressful times, but most teachers say that the more disciplined and regular your meditation, the more value you will get from it. Experiment with various ways of meditating until you find the practice that is right for you.

Find a comfortable sitting position. You might sit on the floor or in a straight chair, but stay away from beds and couches—they will make it difficult for you to sit up straight, with a straight, relaxed spine.

Begin to breathe deeply and slowly and continue to breathe with a slow, deep rhythm. Stare at a single blank spot or close your eyes; avoid looking at a picture, clock, or any other object, since the idea is to clear your mind, not to fill it up with a particular picture.

Then pick one word or phrase and think it over and over again to yourself. Some meditators use "Om"; others are more comfortable with the phrase "I am"; still others like to choose a word that means something to them, such as *beauty, life,* or *love.* Whatever you choose, keep repeating the word in your mind. By repeating this one word, you are allowing your mind to free itself of all other thoughts.

If your mind wanders, allow it to wander, then bring it back and begin again. It takes practice to concentrate on a single word for 10 or 20 minutes! Likewise, if you find yourself falling asleep, use your deep breathing to wake yourself up. Continue to focus on the word or syllable you have chosen. You might want to set an alarm or timer so you don't have to wonder about how long 10 minutes is, but if possible, use your "inner clock" instead.

Many people find that meditation helps them wake up. They recommend it as a substitute for caffeine in the midst of a long study session. Since caffeine makes you anxious while meditation calms you down, it might be worth a try.

Comforts and Rewards

Sometimes, the best way to deal with anxiety is on a totally practical level. Make yourself more comfortable, improve your environment, or give yourself a treat. You might find that the simple process of taking care of yourself helps to calm you down!

Here are some suggestions:

- *Clean your room.* Is your desk a pile of messy papers and your closet a nest of tangled clothes? No wonder you're uneasy! Put on some soothing or energizing music and get to work clearing off and organizing your table tops, sorting through and organizing your closets. You'd be surprised at how much influence a calming environment can have.
- *Peaceful surroundings.* For a special treat in a clean room, add a few more soothing touches. Buy an environmental tape, a calming record of New Age music (available in local New Age bookstores or health food stores), or any other music you find soothing. Turn down the lights and burn a scented candle or incense (always being careful of fire). Get your family to cooperate in giving you an uninterrupted hour of privacy and peace.
- *A hot bath.* If you find water relaxing, pamper yourself in the tub. Buy bath salts, bubble bath, or special soaps. Get

a loofah (a rough sponge) to scrub yourself with. Find a soft robe to wear afterward. Let bathtime become a ritual and a reward. When you go into the bathroom, tell yourself that you are leaving all your worries outside. You might even picture yourself storing your worries in a bag that you leave outside the bathroom.

- *A good book.* Sometimes an absorbing book is the best escape from anxiety. Instead of trying to work out your problems, give yourself a night off from them. Lose yourself in a fantasy novel, a book of science-fiction, or a mystery. Make sure to choose a book that really will allow you to escape, rather than one that worries you further about crime, space invaders, or the lack of romance in your own life!

Food and Exercise

We're used to thinking of anxiety as a state of mind, but sometimes it stems from physical causes, too. Regular aerobic exercise (exercise that involves your breathing and circulatory system) can be a great calming influence. It's best if you exercise vigorously for 20 to 30 minutes, four or five times a week. It's also possible to turn to exercise at those times when you feel especially anxious.

Here are some aerobic exercises that may help keep you calm—as well as fit!

- a brisk walk
- jogging or running
- dancing (if you move continuously for 20 or 30 minutes)
- aerobics
- jumping rope
- exercise bicycling
- swimming

Although long bike rides are technically not considered aerobic exercise because of the many breaks you get when coasting, many people find that bicycling is great for soothing anxious feelings and bringing new perspectives. Likewise, skating, tennis, squash, racquetball, and other vigorous activities can be wonderful anti-anxiety "medications."

Low-Stress and High-Stress Foods

Along with exercise, food can have a major impact on your state of mind. Foods that help weaken your resistance to anxiety include caffeine (found in coffee, tea, chocolate, and colas), sugar (or any sweet foods), and white flour (or any baked goods made with white flour). Foods that help to calm you down include turkey, low-fat dairy products, dark green leafy vegetables (spinach, kale, parsley, kohlrabi, collards and other greens), and whole grains (brown rice, oatmeal, cornmeal, barley, and whole wheat in the form of bread or other baked goods).

As we have said, alcohol, nicotine, and drugs ultimately help create anxiety, even if they seem to temporarily relieve anxious feelings. If you have developed an addiction to liquor, drugs, or cigarettes, you will probably face an anxious time when you stop using them as your body readjusts. A doctor or nutritionist can help you combat this anxiety with diet and exercise.

To some people vitamin B complex, calcium supplements, and iron pills seem helpful in combating anxiety. Take them regularly or on the days when you feel anxious (but no more than one of each vitamin per day!).

If you are seriously concerned about anxiety and your diet, work with a doctor or nutritionist to make the changes that you need. You also might try cutting out all caffeine, processed sugar and sweetened foods, nicotine, alcohol, and drugs for two weeks—just as an experiment. At first, you may have a negative reaction of being excessively tired or craving sweets, but then you may also discover that you begin to tap new reserves of energy and calm.

Mind Boosts

As we have seen, anxiety comes from buried feelings and from certain types of thoughts and attitudes. Sometimes, it's helpful to deal with these feelings and attitudes to combat anxiety.

Feel the Feelings

Getting in touch with the feelings that are buried underneath our anxiety may be one way to relieve our anxious feelings. Sometimes it's enough just to ask yourself, "What am I feeling?" and an answer will pop into your head: "I'm angry with my mother for treating me like a baby again!" "I'm sad that my boyfriend didn't send me a birthday card." "I feel guilty about not walking Sandy home from school when she asked me to."

If you don't get an immediate answer to your question, you might keep asking yourself more specific questions. "Am I angry? Sad? Guilty? What about? Who with?" Keep probing to see if anything pops into your mind.

Another approach to connecting with your feelings is to use visualization. If possible, give yourself a five-minute "time out" in a private and comfortable place—even if you have to run off to a bathroom and shut yourself in a stall!

Get as comfortable as you can and begin your deep breathing. Continuing your rhythm of slow, regular breathing throughout this exercise. Quickly run through muscle relaxation from your toes to your scalp. Then say to yourself, "I am going to have an image that will tell me about my feelings."

Allow an image to come into your mind. Stick with it. Watch it for clues and allow it to change or develop. You might find that the image triggers a new insight, or it may be that simply having the image helps you relax and feel calmer and more connected. You may find the image triggers a powerful feeling of sadness, anger, or guilt, with no explanation, replacing your anxiety with a new feeling.

Some people find it helpful to write or draw about the image they create. Others simply remember it and go on with their day. You may also find it helpful to think about the image just before you fall asleep; you may find yourself dreaming about it, learning still more about your buried thoughts and feelings.

Put Boundaries on It

Sometimes it's helpful simply to acknowledge that you are feeling anxious while focusing on the limits to that anxiety. You might just say to yourself, "I'm feeling anxious and I am safe," or "I'm feeling anxious and everything is all right." That way, you are both acknowledging that you have an unpleasant feeling, and that the feeling isn't going to kill you or threaten your world, no matter how unpleasant it feels.

Notice that we've phrased these statements in a positive manner ("I am safe" rather than "I'm *not* in danger") and that we've used the word *and* instead of *but.* That's because the goal of this exercise is to think positively and to let your anxiety sit side by side with another reality—that you really *are* all right, no matter how you feel. Phrasing the statement in this way helps you to acknowledge your own strength: you are strong enough to tolerate the unpleasant feeling of anxiety without trying to stuff it away.

Keep a Journal

Some people find it helpful to keep a journal, recording their thoughts, feelings, and dreams. Many people like to keep a journal every day, or often as possible; others save their journal writing for times when they feel anxious, lonely, or especially excited.

You may find it especially helpful to write down your dreams. Many people find that over time, this is a calming practice, even if they do no more than record a few dreams in the five or 10 minutes after they first wake up. Often, dreams are a way of "sending messages" to ourselves, letting ourselves know what we really think about a situation or giving ourselves advice about what to do. So for extra insight into yourself, you might spend some time later that day writing and thinking about what those dreams might mean to you or what feelings or experiences led to those dreams.

When Others Feed Your Anxiety

We've talked quite a bit about what you can do to combat your own anxiety. But what about when others are contributing to it? How do you handle the parents who worry about your grades, the teachers who have "all or nothing" attitudes, or the friends who seem to want you to be perfect?

You'll probably find that the more you get in touch with your feelings and adjust your thoughts to a more positive way of thinking, the less these other people have the power to "get to you." However, we are all affected by other people *some* of the time. Here are some ways that you can more actively protect yourself.

Remember That It's OK to Say No—and Say It!

If you are feeling overworked and overscheduled, remind yourself that you have the right to say no. You do not always have to please other people, put other people first, or be concerned with other people's feelings.

Of course, part of becoming an adult is recognizing that there are times when one genuinely does have obligations, to oneself and to others. Schoolwork, chores at home, or requirements at your job may be genuine responsibilities of yours, and saying "no" may not be a real option—or might cause more problems than it would solve. Likewise, in order to have the relationships you want with friends, families, and the other people in your world, it may be necessary or important to occasionally put others first.

To help yourself sort out the necessary from the unnecessary demands, you might ask yourself the following questions:

- Am I doing this because *I* want to or because someone else wants me to?
- What are the consequences—to me and to others—of saying *no* to this? Am I willing to live with them?
- What are the consequences—to me and to others—of agreeing to do this? Am I willing to live with them?

If you've thought it through and decided that you genuinely want to say no, remember that it's easiest if you can simply say no right away. If you can't bring yourself to do that, tell the person who is asking you to do something that you'll think about it. Then think about it—and say no! If necessary, picture just how difficult your life will be if you say yes. Or picture someone you know who has no trouble whatsoever saying no to others. Think of that person as you stand up for yourself, too.

Forgive Yourself for Not Being Perfect

The next time you feel guilty or anxious about how you've treated someone else, remind yourself that nobody's perfect. Try to separate your feelings about what you did from the reality. Did you actually hurt someone, or did you simply not go along with the other person's wishes? Do *you* think you did the right thing, even if the other person doesn't like it? Are your feelings about what you "should" have done based on the idea that you are never allowed to say no, to disagree, or to disappoint somebody else?

If after all this thinking, you're still genuinely sorry about what you did, apologize for it and decide what you'll do next time to take better care of yourself and to ensure that you do what you believe is right. Then allow yourself to forget the situation and move on.

Protect Yourself from Anxiety

What about those conversations with other people that leave you feeling anxious and upset? How should you deal with them?

The first step is to distinguish between constructive and non-constructive criticism. *Constructive criticism* is criticism that can help you. Such criticism is usually given out of a genuine desire to assist, comfort, or suggest new options. Because you may often find it painful to change your behavior or to look critically at what you are doing, constructive criticism may indeed provoke your anxiety, while also being extremely useful to you. If a teacher suggests that you have an unexpected talent for drama, for example, or points out that if you worked harder at French, you might get an A, this may make you feel nervous, worried, or guilty. It may also inspire you to new achievements.

Likewise, if a friend points out that you seem to be extremely touchy whenever a particular subject comes up, or that you are almost always late for your times together, you may feel anxious having your behavior commented on in this way. You may also be able to use the criticism constructively, helping yourself to gain new insights into what you do and how you feel.

On the other hand, teachers, friends, family, and other people in your world may be giving you *nonconstructive criticism* or finding a way to share their own anxieties with you. Nonconstructive criticism may also be given out of a genuine desire to help. The parent who worries about whether you have worked hard enough at your homework or the friend who is nervous about your plan to ask out the attractive new student may be genuinely concerned for your well-being. At the same time, their concerns may not be *your* concerns, and their fears may not necessarily be appropriate for you.

Sometimes, too, nonconstructive criticism comes out of more complicated motives. A person who is envious of you may express his or her envy as concern that you may fail. A person who is angry with you may not express that anger directly, but rather as criticism of some other part of your behavior about which you are feeling especially vulnerable. A younger brother or sister, for example, may envy you the greater freedom of your social life or be angry with you for seeming more interested in your friends and the people you date than in him or her. This sibling may even be able to point out something that sounds true ("Gee, Sandy hasn't called you at all this week. What do you think that means?" or "Boy, those pants make you look really fat!"). True or not, the criticism is not constructive because it isn't coming from a genuine desire to help, but rather from the desire to make you feel anxious.

One way to protect yourself from anxiety, then, is to distinguish between constructive and nonconstructive criticism. If criticism seems not only true, but useful, you can decide what action to take as a result—try out for a play, study harder, examine a particularly touchy subject, or make a greater effort to be on time. If there is nothing you can do about the criticism except worry and feel bad about it, that's probably nonconstructive criticism, even if some aspects of it sound true.

If someone seems to want to have a conversation with you about a topic that makes you anxious, decide whether you genuinely have anything to gain from listening and being open. If you decide that you do not, find a way to end the conversation or change the subject. Don't argue; you probably won't be able to convince the other person to think differently. Instead, find a polite way to acknowledge the other person's concern and then change the subject.

Try using sentences like, "Maybe you're right; I'll think about what you've said," or "Thanks for your concern; by the way, what about . . . " Don't feel obligated to explain your feelings or to hear the other person out a second time. Instead, find a way to stay centered on what *you* think is best while ending a conversation that is only going to upset you.

Start Expressing Your Feelings

If you are angry, sad, or disappointed in someone else, you might begin expressing those feelings to the person in question. Once you stop trying to hide your "bad" feelings, you might find yourself feeling a lot less anxious.

It is often better not to express your feelings as criticism or as a demand ("How dare you stand me up like that!" "I insist you give me back my book right away!"). You may simply say something like, "I felt terrible when you couldn't come with me yesterday," or "It made me really mad when you forgot to give me back my book."

It may help to end such a statement with a question, asking the other person how he or she thinks the two of you should handle such situations in the future or making a suggestion of your own: "Next time, would you give me more notice when you have to break a date?" "How can we make sure that I get my things back when I lend them to you?"

If you have rarely expressed such feelings in the past, people may be surprised when you begin to do so now. Stick to your guns—you'll find that sooner or later, people will like you better and treat you better now that you're sticking up for yourself! And you'll find that you're enjoying your friendships more—besides feeling a whole lot less anxious!

4

Depression

James seems to have it made. He's a straight-A student, his family is well-off and treats him well, he's popular in school and good at sports. Although James doesn't have a steady girlfriend, he has no trouble finding attractive, popular girls to go out with. He's been accepted into the college of his choice, where he plans to study pre-law, and he's even landed a summer job at a law firm. Yet despite all of these positive things, James is finding it harder and harder to get through each day. Nothing really seems to matter very much. Even little things that he used to enjoy—a favorite walk home from school, a funny movie, a pizza with extra cheese—don't seem to give him much pleasure anymore. Increasingly, James feels as though there's a glass wall between him and the rest of the world, so that he can't touch others or be touched by them. Although no one seems to suspect that anything is wrong, James himself feels as though he's just going through the motions—and he's beginning to wonder whether things will ever get better.

Tanya feels like she's always on a roller coaster. Some days she's on top of the world and everything seems possible. Other days, she hates herself: She feels fat, ugly, stupid, and doomed to a horrible life where nothing ever works out. Some days she's grateful for her friends and family, who are so wonderful, and other days she feels like nobody loves her and the people she knows aren't worth loving anyway. The "down" days really scare Tanya, and she's starting to feel like she'll do anything to get away from that "down" feeling. Sometimes she tries doing something really wild, like drag racing or going to a dangerous part of the city and seeing if she can get a bar to serve her. Lately, it seems like the only times she can stand herself is when she's either drunk or high and the "down" feelings go away for a little while—until the next day. Then they come back, stronger than ever—and Tanya feels even more desperate.

Lisa, whom we met in Chapter 2, has felt worried and anxious for a long time. Lately, though, she's felt too tired to worry. Instead, she just feels hopeless. Nothing seems to comfort her. Lisa used to eat because she felt worried and it calmed her down. Now she eats because eating special treats seems like the one nice thing she can count on. But even food doesn't taste as good to her as it used to. Lisa feels tired a lot of the time, as though she barely has the energy to get out of bed in the morning or to get herself to school and back. She's been sick a lot, too—little things, like sore throats and headaches, as well as a couple of severe colds and cases of the flu with a high fever. Sometimes, the smallest thing can make her cry, like a television commercial about a parent and child who are separated. Other times, it seems like she could hear the worst news in the world and she wouldn't even have the energy to get upset. Lisa feels like she's living inside a damp, gray cloud that she carries with her wherever she goes.

What Is Depression?

James, Tanya, and Lisa are all suffering from depression. Depression can be difficult to understand. We're likely to confuse it with feeling sad, grieving, or having a hard time. Depression can go along with those conditions, but it's possible to be sad without being depressed—and it's possible to be depressed for no apparent reason. Like anxiety, depression is a complicated emotional state that isn't always easy to explain at first glance.

People can be depressed in many different ways. Sometimes you might know that you're depressed. Someone you love has died, or broken up with you, or moved away. You didn't do well on an important test, or in an important game. You've made specific plans and they haven't worked out, or you're not getting along with someone in your family. All these things can feel "depressing," in different ways and to different degrees.

Other times, you don't really know why you're feeling the way you do. All you know is that you're not feeling much of anything. You don't feel like doing the things you usually do—you may even not feel like getting out of bed in the morning. Life seems dull or feels like an impossibly heavy burden. Food doesn't taste good; sleep doesn't come easily; friends aren't as much fun as they usually are.

The dictionary defines *depression* in two different ways. One definition is how we usually use the term: "low spirits; gloominess; dejection; sadness." The other speaks to a more serious problem: "an emotional condition . . . characterized by feelings of hopelessness, inadequacy, etc."

As we've said, everyone feels "blue"—in low spirits, gloomy, dejected, or sad—some of the time. The problem comes when these low spirits last for days, weeks, or even longer—or when they come back for a couple of days a week, every week. Someone who is in low spirits for long periods at a time, or on a regular basis, may be suffering from *depression*. In that case, the "blues" are probably accompanied by deeper feelings of hopelessness and inadequacy as the depressed person struggles to keep going somehow in the face of despair.

Understanding Depression

Depression is the subject of a great deal of controversy among doctors, psychiatrists, and psychologists. Part of the controversy stems from a confusion about the word *depression* itself, as we have just seen. To help clarify this issue, we find it helpful to talk about three different types of depression. If after reading our descriptions you are concerned about how they apply to you or someone you know, find a doctor, psychologist, or counselor whom you trust and discuss your concerns.

As we have seen, one type of depression may be seen as just the *low spirits* that occasionally plague all of us. This response may have psychological roots: You're worried, frightened, angry, or have suffered a loss. It may also be connected to a physical cause, such as lack of sleep, certain factors in your diet, a medication or birth-control pills, or the weather. (For more information on these issues, see "Other Causes of Depression," below.)

Sometimes depression is *set off by a life event,* such as a death; a move to another place; a break-up with a boyfriend, girlfriend, or close friend; or a parent's divorce or remarriage. In such cases, the event might produce strong feelings of loss, grief, anger, and despair. It might also set off other feelings that have been buried for a long time. For example, if a boy's mother died when the boy was five, the painful feelings of losing one's mother might have been too much for the five-year-old to handle. But when, at age 15, the boy's father remarries and moves to another city, the boy experiences, not only a reaction to those specific events, but also some of the feelings that go back to his mother's death. It's usually those "extra " buried feelings that make the difference between the normal period of grief, anger, and readjustment and the paralyzing feeling of depression.

Finally, there is the condition that psychologists refer to as *major depression* or *clinical depression.* Although no one has fully been able to explain this type of depression, most doctors and psychiatrists theorize that this condition has biological roots, related to a person's brain chemistry and possibly also related to hormonal activity. Thus a person who is prone to clinical depression might not discover it until the teen years, when new hormonal activity begins.

The main distinction between clinical depression and other types of depression is that no life event seems to account for why the clinically depressed person would feel bad. Scientists theorize that this is because the depressed feelings have their source in biological problems, not emotional ones. On the other hand, feeling bad much of the time can create emotional problems of its own. In addition, a person may have both biological and psychological reasons to feel depressed. And of course, a person who "seems" to have "no reason" to feel depressed may have a very good reason. As we saw in the last two chapters, Lisa seems to have a happy, loving family, as she would be the first to tell a counselor. Yet the gap between the reality and Lisa's picture of it is exactly what makes Lisa feel depressed.

Following are the standards recommended by the American Psychological Association to determine if an adult is suffering from major depression. To be given this diagnosis, a person must not be taking any medication, drugs or alcohol that might account for these reactions; must not have suffered a particular loss or letdown (such as the end of a particularly intense period of work, a break-up, or the death of a loved one) that would account for feeling bad; and must experience a depressed mood plus a minimum of four of the following symptoms for a minimum of two weeks:

- less or no interest in things previously pleasurable
- unintentional weight loss or gain
- insomnia (inability to sleep) or hypersomnia (desire to sleep more than usual)
- agitated or depressed motor actions; that is, an outsider can observe that the person moves more jerkily or more slowly than usual
- persistent loss of energy or fatigue
- feelings of worthlessness sometimes accompanied by delusions or hallucinations
- diminished ability to think clearly
- many thoughts of death or suicide

There seems to be an inherited predisposition to clinical depression, which means that if someone in your family suffers from this syndrome, you may also be vulnerable to it. No one can fully agree on exactly what causes this condition or how to treat it, but antidepressant medication often proves helpful. Unlike tranquilizers, such medication does not affect a person's functioning or alter a mood but rather attempts to correct the brain and body chemistry.

The focus of this and the next chapter will be on depression whose cause is not primarily biological. If you believe that you or someone you know is suffering from clinical depression, see a doctor, psychologist, or counselor to discuss your concerns.

Identifying Depression

There are many ways to recognize the state of depression. Here are some signs:

- Frequently feeling tired, listless, low-energy
- Loss of appetite or hugely increased appetite
- Loss of interest in a physical relationship—or sudden interest only in the physical side of the relationship
- Lack of enjoyment in things that used to give pleasure, such as sports, movies, time with friends
- Feeling "flat" or "blah," without much interest in anything or response to anything
- A frequent or constant state of hopelessness or despair
- Crying jags or frequently being moved to tears very easily
- Headaches
- A sense of isolation—the feeling that nobody understands or cares, the feeling that you "can't get through" to anybody
- Lack of interest in your physical appearance, or being overly preoccupied with your physical appearance in a negative way
- Sleeping badly

- Sleeping more than usual
- Feeling as though the bad feelings have always been there, or as though they will never go away; not being able to imagine feeling any other way
- Thoughts of death, such as picturing how peaceful death might be, or imagining how sorry everyone else will be once you've died

Not everyone who is depressed experiences all of these things. And everyone experiences some of them some of the time. If many of the items on this list describe you or someone you know *most* of the time, however, or if you or someone you know feels this way *regularly*, you or your friend is probably suffering from some form of depression and would benefit from learning more about where the depression is coming from and how to cope with it, and should probably seek professional help.

What Causes Depression?

All people get depressed from time to time—especially when they're teenagers. That's because one reason for depression is buried feelings, and the teen years are a time when buried feelings often rise to the surface. Let's say that you've had a terrible loss in your life—a loved person has died, moved away, or started to treat you differently. Or you may have lost a beloved pet, moved away from a favorite spot, or passed out of the grade of a favorite teacher.

At the time, this loss was very painful. It made you very sad to lose the person you loved, and it made you angry that you couldn't do anything about it. You might have been uncomfortable feeling so sad, or so angry, and therefore, to protect yourself, you tried to stuff those feelings away.

In a way, you built defenses—walls to hide your feelings. One defense might be, "I don't really care—I didn't like that person much anyway." Or you might defend yourself by saying, "I felt a little unhappy about it, but I don't mind now." These defenses helped you deal with a difficult situation— but at the price of stuffing your emotions away. And emotions don't really go away until you feel them fully. They only go into hiding.

Now that you're a teenager, your body is changing very quickly. Changes in hormones, body chemistry, and body weight make it more difficult for you to keep up your defenses. The walls you built come tumbling down, and all those difficult feelings come flooding back.

Of course, even if your feelings come back, you don't necessarily recognize them. That's why there may be days when you're very upset and you don't know why. You may be experiencing a feeling about something that happened to you a long time ago. You still have the feeling, even though you can't remember the reason for it. Or you may get very sad or very angry about some little thing that doesn't seem that important, even to you. That may be because you're actually sad or angry about something else, and this new incident is simply bringing up those old feelings that didn't come out before.

Sometimes your buried feelings don't go back to the past. They may have their source right here in the present. If your parents are divorcing, for example, you may be very angry with them for not being able to get along. At the same time, your mind may understand that your parents aren't really doing anything "wrong." You feel guilty being angry at your mother when she's trying so hard. Or you're uncomfortable feeling sad about your father when you're supposed to be grown up and not need him any more. So you try to bury these feelings, too.

But buried feelings always come back. Maybe you can't get angry with your mother for divorcing your father—but perhaps you find yourself blowing up at her for forgetting to wash your socks. Maybe you're not comfortable being sad about your father—but you spend three days crying over that B-minus on your math test.

Sooner or later, buried feelings will work their way to the surface. If you find that every so often, you're sad, or depressed, and don't know why, it's not really something to worry about. But if your depressions are lasting for more than about 10 days, or if you're seriously depressed for a day or two each week, then you may want to look more closely at what's going on. You may have some feelings that you're not dealing with, some feelings that need your attention.

What are the kinds of buried feelings that can turn into depression? Interestingly, they are many of the same feelings that can turn into anxiety: anger, guilt, and sadness. Any feeling that you are not comfortable with and try to "pretend away" may come back in the form of either anxiety or depression.

James, for example, feels a great deal of pressure from his parents to always put a happy face on things. Ever since he was a little boy, he realized that his parents became extremely upset if he was having a hard time with anything. His father would become anxious and nervous and would perhaps get angry and try to blame a teacher or a friend of James's for the problem. His mother would offer James one solution after another, waiting for James to pick the one that he thought would work. James got the message that when he got upset, his parents got even more upset than he did!

So James learned how to handle his own problems and to hide his difficulties from his parents. But since James has problems like everybody else, pretending that everything is always fine puts him under an enormous strain. That makes him angry. Since he doesn't feel comfortable expressing that anger to his parents—or even feeling it himself—James has started to turn off *all* his feelings. Since he can't express his anger directly—by yelling or explaining how he feels, or even by punching a pillow and yelling at his parents in his head—he expresses his anger indirectly—by keeping his parents at a distance, feeling as though there's a glass wall between him and them. The only problem is, James doesn't get to feel any of his feelings, and the "glass wall" keeps everyone else away, too.

Tanya is trying to bury her feelings of being lonely and sad. When she was 13, Tanya's family moved to a new city, and Tanya never quite managed to fit in with her new surroundings. The next year, Tanya's grandmother, with whom she was very close, died. To Tanya, losing her friends and her grandmother in such a short time was too much to handle. To protect herself from the pain, she tried to bury it. But the sad and lonely feelings keep coming back. Instead of feeling those feelings and working them through, Tanya keeps trying to push them away by doing dangerous things or by numbing herself with drugs or alcohol.

As we've seen, anxiety works in a similar way—it comes from buried feelings that a person is trying not to have. In fact, anxious people are often depressed as well, or go back and forth between being anxious and being depressed. Lisa is one of those people. As we saw in Chapter 2, Lisa's family acts as though they love her very much, but Lisa's experience is that they aren't really there for her. Since it's too frightening to admit that her parents don't really love her, Lisa tries to push those feelings away. Sometimes the buried feelings come back as anxiety, sometimes they come back as depression. As long as Lisa tries to bury them, they'll come back somehow.

Depression and Women

Although anyone can be depressed, it seems that a higher percentage of depressed people are female. There are many reasons for this, but psychologists believe one key reason is that women in our society are especially encouraged to bury their feelings of anger, aggressiveness, and care for themselves. Instead of expressing feelings and feeling comfortable with them, girls and women often feel that they must be nice, pleasant, happy, smiling, and unselfish all of the time. So the buried feelings that they think are not so nice get directed against themselves—as depression.

For example, if a girl's boyfriend breaks up with her because he wants to go out with someone else, a girl may become extremely depressed. Of course, anyone would be sad about losing someone they love. But when the sadness becomes depression, we might ask what buried feelings are not being expressed.

Many psychologists would say that a girl in this situation might also be very angry with her boyfriend. But because "nice girls" aren't supposed to get angry, the girl may not be comfortable with saying, "What a rotten thing to do! He's acting like a terrible person and I hope he's miserable!" She may be more comfortable saying, "Oh, I love him so much— I can't believe he doesn't love me anymore. I wish he'd change his mind—I'd love him so much if he came back."

Likewise, many girls are not comfortable saying "no" to people who ask them for help. If a girl is already taking a full load of classes, studying music, and working on the school paper, she may have enough to do—but feels too guilty to say so when the drama club comes to ask her to run lights for their latest production. Instead of simply saying "no," the girl may find some way to fit this new demand into her schedule—but her secret anger about doing too much may come back as depression.

Attitudes That Feed Depression

As with anxiety, certain mental attitudes can help feed depression. In fact, many of the same attitudes that help create anxiety also help create depression. These attitudes have to do with expecting others to be perfect, expecting oneself to be perfect, focusing on the negative instead of on the positive, focusing on the past or the future instead of on the present, and focusing on others at the expense of yourself.

Here are some examples of these attitudes. How many of them do you recognize?

Expecting Others to Be Perfect

Tanya's best friend, Libby, is preoccupied and distant on a day that Tanya is feeling "down." Tanya tries three times to tell her friend about an argument she had with her math teacher, but the friend doesn't seem very interested and finally says, "Oh, Tanya, give me a break! Who cares, anyway?"

Anyone might be hurt or annoyed at this response to a problem from a good friend. But Tanya has a hard time saying, "Well, Libby must be having problems of her own. I guess she can't think about me right now." Tanya also has a hard time saying, "Libby, I know you're upset, but I'm having a hard day, too." Instead, Tanya retreats into herself, feeling hurt, lonely, and more sure than ever that nobody loves her. Tanya has a hard time accepting that Libby can't be the "perfect" friend who is always available and never loses her temper—even though she can still be a good friend who most of the time is there for Tanya.

Expecting Oneself to Be Perfect

The night before his first day on his new job, James goes out with a couple of friends. They stay out much later than James had planned, and the next morning, James oversleeps. He arrives for his first day at work tired, messily dressed—and late. Nobody says anything to him directly, but James is sure that his new boss and coworkers have lowered their opinions of him.

James definitely made a mistake. It probably wasn't a good idea to stay out late the night before starting a new job. But instead of accepting that he made a mistake and going on, James agonizes over his possible failure. It seems like one more proof that he can't do anything right, that as hard as he tries, somehow, he always messes up. Because James expects himself to be perfect, he doesn't notice the good things he does—after all, they're what he expects—while the mistakes and failures seem gigantic.

Focusing on the Negative Instead of on the Positive

Lisa goes to a party and actually has a pretty good time. She dances with a couple of guys she likes, talks for a few minutes with a girl she's been wanting to meet, and spends some time hanging out with a couple of girls she's known for a while. Then, just before she leaves, she bumps into a guy and spills a coke all over him. Lisa is so embarrassed she wants to sink through the floor. By the time she gets home, she's almost in tears.

Lisa has a hard time staying focused on the nice things that happened on the party. Instead, it's as though the one bad thing that happened wiped out all the good things. Since bad things are always going to happen from time to time, this kind of attitude feeds Lisa's feelings of hopelessness and despair.

Focusing on the Past or the Future Rather than the Present

As James starts his new job, he wants to be very careful to make a good impression, especially after being late that first day. So every day when he gets home from work, James thinks about what he did that day and whether he made the right decision. Was it OK to bring that stuff up from the supply room without asking? Maybe that made his boss mad. But if he *hadn't* brought the stuff up, would he have looked like he didn't know what he was doing? James can think about such things for hours.

When James gets a compliment at work, that doesn't satisfy him. He immediately imagines the mistakes he might make that will show that the compliment isn't true.

Focusing on the past and the future help feed James's sense of hopelessness and despair. After all, it *is* hopeless to change the past. And he *can't* control the future. Focusing on things that he can't affect reinforces James's feeling that nothing he does will make him happy.

Focusing on Others at Your Own Expense

Tanya has a favorite sweater that doesn't fit her anymore but which she loves anyway. Her grandmother gave it to her, and it reminds Tanya of her grandmother.

Tanya's sister wants to wear the sweater, and Tanya's parents try to convince Tanya to give it away, or at least to share it. After all, they point out, it no longer fits Tanya. How can she be so selfish as to keep something that she can't even use?

Tanya feels guilty about feeling selfish and about being so babyish about the sweater, so she gives it to her younger sister. Now she feels terrible. Tanya isn't only missing the sweater, she's angry with her parents, her sister, and herself. Instead of taking care of herself, Tanya did what others wanted her to do—and now she's depressed.

Other Causes of Depression

Buried feelings may be one cause of depression. But there are definitely other causes, as well. As we have seen, some people seem to have a biological tendency to become depressed. If you or someone you know seems seriously depressed all the time, the depression may have a biological cause as well as as psychological one. In this case, professional help should be sought.

Other people are sensitive to certain types of food—or to certain shortages in their diets. A depression may be caused by getting too much of one kind of food, or not enough of another. People who go on crash diets are especially vulnerable to depression, since their bodies aren't getting the nourishment they need to cope with life's demands.

Some people become depressed when they don't get enough sunlight. That's why we tend to think of winter or rainy days as "depressing" times. There is apparently some chemical in the sunlight that is necessary to a good feeling of mental health.

Lack of sleep may contribute to depression, and so might lack of exercise. Certain prescribed medications, drugs, or alcohol contribute to depression in some people. Many girls and women experience depression in relation to their menstrual cycle, usually on the day or week before their periods begin. Because of their relation to hormones, birth control pills can contribute to depression as well.

As you can see, there are many causes of depression, and even scientists don't fully understand them all. If you are concerned about being depressed, finish this chapter and see Chapter 5. Try some of our suggestions for coping or come up with some of your own. But if these suggestions don't work, don't worry. It only means that you need help in locating the causes and solutions to your own particular situation. And, as you can see in Chapter 6, help is available.

When Depression Becomes Fatal: Teenage Suicide

Sometimes depression feels so overwhelming that death may seem like the only way out. As we saw, one of the characteristics of depression is the feeling that things have always been bad and they always will be, the inability to imagine any other feeling than the feeling of being depressed. In those low moments when it seems that life will never get better, suicide may come to seem like a solution.

Of course, not all people who commit suicide suffer from depression. And the vast majority of depressed adults and teens may never even consider suicide as a response to their condition. In many cases, however, depression is an expression of anger that the depressed person feels unable to express. Instead, he or she turns that anger inward, punishing himself or herself by feeling depressed, despairing, or worthless. The extreme expression of punishing oneself in this way is for a person to decide that he or she doesn't deserve to live or that life is so awful that even death must be better.

The past several years have seen a dramatic rise in suicide rates among teenagers. Since 1955, the suicide rate in the United States has gone up more than 300 percent, and just between 1960 and 1980, the rate went up 136 percent. Some 6,000 teenagers commit suicide every year.

The National Committee on Suicide Youth Prevention estimates that over half a million teenagers try to kill themselves each year. Other experts estimate that there are actually 2 million attempts and almost 25,000 suicides, according to Dr. Miriam Adderholdt-Elliot's book *Perfectionism, What's Bad About Being Too Good.*

Enough teenagers kill themselves each year to make suicide the third leading cause of death among U.S. residents between the ages of 15 and 24. Although many of these deaths are unexpected, there are some warning signs.

Warning Signs of Suicide

- Withdrawal and isolation; lack of contact with family and friends
- Withdrawal from school or other social activities
- Sudden unexplained changes in personality, appetite, sleeping habits, schoolwork, or behavior
- Drug or alcohol abuse
- Continual boredom, listlessness, lack of ability to have fun
- Loss of interest in grooming, dress, and appearance
- Trouble with concentration
- Illnesses with no apparent cause

- Severe depression of a week or longer
- Some form of suicide threat, discussions of suicide or death, preoccupation with death, repeated jokes about suicide and death
- Saying goodbye to family and friends, giving away possessions, making preparations to "wind things up"

If these signs apply to you or to anyone you know, *get help*. Tell a sympathetic adult, call a hot line, or find a counseling service. You can also turn to Chapter 6 for more information on coping with depression, and to Chapter 7 for some hot line and national resource numbers.

Coping with Depression

Everyone experiences periods of feeling down. And we've all said, or heard somebody say, "I'm depressed." There are lots of different ways of feeling "depressed," and lots of different ways of responding to the feeling.

Sometimes depression goes away by itself. Sometimes family or friends can help intervene; sometimes there are ways we can cope with depression by ourselves. Sometimes we need more help, such as counseling.

While it's continuing, depression can feel overwhelming and permanent. But it doesn't have to be. The more you learn about yourself and your feelings, the better your chances of coping with depression.

5

Coping with Depression

The problem with depression is that while you're in the midst of it, it feels overwhelming. It may seem as though you've never felt any other way. Certainly it seems as though you never *will* feel any other way. Many people, especially those who have been severely depressed or depressed over long periods of time, describe it as a feeling without boundaries that seems to spread over every area of their lives so that nothing seems untouched by this horrible cloud.

Another difficult thing about depression is that it can feel like a moral failing—something that is your fault. You may feel tired and miserable, unable to get out of bed in the morning or incapable of controlling your tears. But you may also feel guilty or ashamed of these feelings, as though you should just "pull yourself together" or "grow up" or "stop being so lazy." Possibly friends or family members have said these things to you while you were depressed, or expressed these attitudes without words. You may even think they're right—but it doesn't help you break out of your depression. In fact, it only makes you feel worse.

If you've felt this way, take heart. Depression doesn't last forever and those gloomy feelings about your life are just that—feelings, not facts. And depression isn't a moral failing or a "fault." It's a condition that most people experience at least some of the time, a condition common to teenagers, with both physical and psychological roots. In this chapter, we'll give you some suggestions for coping with your depression or with the depressions of others. If these suggestions don't work, turn to Chapters 6 and 7 for other ideas about how to get help. But don't give up—and don't blame yourself. The first step to coping with depression is to accept your feelings without blame or judgment and start to get the help and comfort that you deserve.

Let's Get Practical

There are lots of ways to cope with a mild depression—a passing case of the blues, or a few "down" days. Here are a few suggestions to try for those times when you're feeling sad or empty or lonely and don't quite know why.

Exercise

The very best single cure for this kind of depression is exercise. Exercise—particularly vigorous aerobic exercise— helps the body produce *endorphins,* chemicals that are natural antidepressants. Thus there is a very good physical reason why you will find yourself feeling happier after a brisk walk or a hard run, not to mention the general increase in your physical fitness and sense of well-being.

To work, the exercise should be regular, at least four or five times a week. You may notice a lift in mood right away, or it may take a week or so to make a change, so keep at it. Aerobic exercise most likely to produce endorphins includes brisk walking, jogging, running, exercise bicycling, continuous dancing, swimming, and aerobic exercise classes. Bicycling, skating, tennis, squash, basketball, and other vigorous sports aren't quite as good, because they don't usually provide the magic 20–30 minutes of continuous motion (usually they feature vigorous activity interspersed with short rests), but they can also be useful in combating depression, particularly if you enjoy them.

Yoga, modern dance, weight lifting, and other less aerobic and sometimes less vigorous forms of exercise are also useful, though they don't contribute to the production of endorphins in quite the same way. However, the sense of physical well-being and body awareness that they promote also helps combat depression.

Diet

Did you know that some foods actually help contribute to depression in some people? And that alcohol, which most people think makes them feel "good," is actually a depressant?

If you are feeling down and don't know why, what you are eating and drinking may have something to do with it. The biggest culprit is processed sugar and all sweetened foods, including those sweetened with honey, corn syrup, fructose, and molasses (this includes a lot of so-called health desserts!). Another substance that can promote depression is caffeine, found in coffee, tea, some sodas, and chocolate.

How does this work? When the body absorbs any kind of food, it converts the food into blood sugar. Then it releases a substance called insulin to convert the blood sugar into energy. When your blood sugar level is high, you feel full of energy. When your blood sugar level is low, you feel tired and hungry.

When you eat something sweet, your blood sugar level goes up very quickly. That's why you feel a jolt of energy, a rush, or a sugar high. But this extra blood sugar stimulates an extra production of insulin—so much so, that even more blood sugar than usual is processed. The result is that your blood sugar level drops very quickly, so that the sugar high is followed by a sugar crash. This crash can help keep a depression going.

Ironically, when your energy is low, you may crave sugar or sweet foods, especially if you are used to eating them. And if you eat something sweet, you may feel satisfied—but only for a short time, while your blood sugar level is high. Pretty soon, it comes crashing down and you feel low again.

Caffeine creates a similar high-crash effect. You drink a cola or a cup of coffee and feel wide awake, happy, and alert. Soon, however, as the caffeine leaves your system, you feel low and groggy. You may crave even more caffeine at such a time—but that will only keep the cycle going. Caffeine also destroys vitamin B, which your body uses to combat stress—and which might help you keep from turning stress into depression.

If you are feeling depressed and low-energy, try switching your diet. Cut out all sugar and sweetened foods, as well as all caffeine. You may feel better immediately or for a week or two, you may feel worse, as your body goes into withdrawal and you miss these substances. (If this happens, you may want to cut caffeine out gradually rather than quit cold-turkey. You might also want to take some vitamin B complex at the times when you especially crave caffeine, although you should take no more than one vitamin B pill a day.) Within a month, you will probably discover that you have a great deal more energy than you did before, and that you no longer crash into depression as easily as you once did.

Good foods for combating depression are whole grains and food made of them (rice, barley, whole-wheat bread), fish, turkey, and green leafy vegetables (spinach, kale, collard greens). A diet rich in B vitamins, calcium, and iron is also good for combating depression. In addition, those foods make up a very low-fat diet, which puts less strain on your system.

You might also cut out all alcohol for a few weeks to see if that has any impact on your bad moods. Alcohol is full of sugar, creating a similar high-crash cycle as the one we described with processed sugar. (If you find it upsetting or difficult to go without drinking—or even to imagine doing so—you may have developed an addiction to alcohol. Call one of the resources in Chapter 7 for help!) Likewise, you might cut out any drug use, since many drugs are either depressants (marijuana, tranquilizers) or stimulants that leave you feeling crashed afterward (cocaine, amphetamines).

In all of these cases—diet, drinking, and drugs—it's probably most useful to experiment with these changes for a month, so that you can really see what their effects are on you. Then you can modify your habits as necessary. For example, you might decide that it's all right to indulge in sweets occasionally, but choose to stay away from them when other events are bringing you down, knowing that they'll help bring you lower. (You may find that giving up drugs or alcohol for a couple of weeks makes it easier to give them up altogether.)

Sleep

Sometimes depression can simply be caused by lack of sleep. If you're feeling blue, check to make sure you're getting the number of hours each night that are right for you. Most people need eight or nine hours, although some people can do well on six or seven. You may be functioning but still not be well rested—you might experiment with adding hours of sleep and seeing if you become more cheerful.

It may also be that you're not getting enough rest from the sleep you do get. Again, cutting caffeine and/or processed sugar from your diet will help you to sleep more deeply. Some people find that taking a hot bath before bed helps them relax. Others enjoy reading quietly or listening to some soothing music. Find a way to let go of the troubles and cares of your day before you go to bed. Exercising right before bed is usually not a very good idea since it is likely to wake you up.

It may also be helpful to go to bed at a different time. Some people feel better going to bed early and getting up early, while other people do better with a later schedule. Modify and experiment with yours, to the extent that school, job, and family will allow.

Generally, you'll feel more rested if you don't eat for two hours before going to bed. Sleep is your body's time for restoring itself—if you ask your body to digest food as well, you're distracting it from its job of getting rest.

Improve Your Surroundings

Sometimes an action as simple as cleaning your room can help bring you out of a bad mood. For one thing, you're now focused on an activity, not on how bad you feel. For another, you're doing something loving to take care of yourself, which is always a good thing. And you're also making a definite improvement in your surroundings, which, small as it may seem, helps to remind you that you are not completely powerless. No matter what else is going wrong, at least you can control *this* part of your life!

Some people enjoy finding some way to improve their environments when they're depressed. If your room is already clean, think about what you could do to make it more comfortable. Maybe you could buy yourself some flowers, or a new tape to play, or a scented candle to burn. Perhaps you could change a poster, or rearrange the books on your shelves, or reorganize your desk. If these projects seem overwhelming to you in your down mood, think of some very small thing that you might do easily—and then do it! You'll be surprised at how much difference it can make to do something as simple as sweeping the floor or wiping the dust off your stereo.

Do Something Nice for Yourself

Caring for yourself when you feel that no one else cares for you can help turn your feelings around. It's an act of faith, so don't think about it—just find something positive to do, and do it! Prepare a favorite meal, sit down with a great romance or mystery novel, make a call to a special friend or relative, take a trip to a special place like a park or a museum.

Get a Change of Scene

Get out of the environment that's bringing you down and escape for a while. Go to a movie, take a walk, get out of town for a day if possible. Sometimes all you need to get a new perspective is to be somewhere else.

Talk to Someone

One of the worst parts of feeling depressed can be that feeling that you can't reach anyone or that no one cares about you. Prove to yourself that that isn't true. Find a friend or a sympathetic adult to talk to. Or start a cheerful, casual conversation with a stranger—a waitress or a store clerk— just to remind yourself that you *can* connect.

Indulge Your Feelings

Maybe what you really need is to feel depressed for a while. Go ahead—give in to it. Put on a mournful record, write in your journal, spend the day in bed, cry. Ironically, it can be a wonderful feeling to just give in to feeling bad.

If you do this frequently, or use it as a way to avoid people or responsibilities, then you might want to find other ways of coping. But for those occasional times of feeling down, it might be just what you need.

If It Doesn't Go Away

What if your down times are lasting more than two or three days? Or what if they're coming frequently, say, one or two bad days each week? The suggestions listed above may help a little bit, or for a little while, but basically, your depression doesn't seem to go away.

First, rule out physical causes. Girls, especially, should check two areas: birth control pills and menstrual cycles. If you are on the pill and you are intensely or frequently depressed, go see your gynecologist. If he or she doesn't take your problem seriously, find another doctor. Even if the pills you are taking aren't the cause of your depression, they may be contributing to it.

If you aren't on the pill, or if your doctor has ruled this out as a possibility, keep a monthly calendar of your ups and downs and compare it with your menstrual cycle. Many women are especially prone to depression the week before or the week of their periods. If you discover such a pattern, you might be especially careful to get enough sleep and exercise, eat low-stress foods, and avoid caffeine, sugar, drugs, and alcohol during those times. Many women also find it helpful to avoid salt when they are pre-menstrual or menstruating. See if such care helps make a dent in your depressions. You might also want to see a doctor who knows about *pre-menstrual syndrome* (the condition of having these problems before your period).

Boys and girls with persistent depression should check with their doctors in any case. Problems with sleep, exercise, or diet may be more serious than you realize, and, when corrected, may also correct your depression. A doctor can also determine whether your depression can be helped with medication.

You may also find that you have a family history of depression. This may sometimes be difficult to determine, since many people who are depressed are never diagnosed as being so. They just seem to be having difficult times, often for apparently good reasons. However, as we have seen, most scientists now believe that some types of depression have biological roots as well as psychological ones. Depression is often associated with migraine headaches, and there is some evidence that both conditions share similar biological roots.

If you are concerned about your depressions, you might want to see a doctor. He or she can work with you to determine what your diet, sleep and exercise patterns, and current medications may have to do with your low moods. Your doctor may also recommend antidepressant medication. This medicine is prescribed on the theory that depression is often caused by an imbalance in body chemistry. Antidepressant medication is quite different from tranquilizers, which alter your mood, and which should not be prescribed to teenagers except in extreme circumstances.

Making It Through the Day

Sometimes the only way to cope with depression is to take it one step at a time. Just making it through the day, knowing that a time will come when the depression lifts, is the best that you can do.

If your depression seems to be lasting longer than it should, we urge you to get help, as described in Chapters 6 and 7. Meanwhile, however, here are some things that you can do to keep yourself going.

Affirmations: Thinking Positively

As we explained in Chapter 3, affirmations are a form of positive thinking that many people find helpful. An affirmation is a positive statement that you repeat in a regular way. Most people find it helpful to repeat affirmations in the morning soon after they get up and in the evening just before they fall asleep. Some people post their affirmations in places where they will see them often, or say their affirmations at particularly stressful or depressing times.

Here are some examples of affirmations that you may find useful:

- I am a wonderful person.
- I am loved and I deserve to be loved.
- My life is rich and full of good things.
- Every day I find some reason to be joyful.
- I am beautiful.
- I am capable.
- Every day I take another step towards achieving my dreams.

At first glance, you might feel silly repeating such statements to yourself, especially if you're feeling low or depressed. You may feel that these statements are not true, so why repeat them?

Interestingly, athletes have found that by giving themselves continual positive reinforcement, their games improve. People recovering from alcohol or drug addictions have also found affirmations useful, as do people struggling with eating disorders. Particularly when you are depressed, it seems more useful to focus on the good than to try to paint an "accurate" overall picture of whether your life is "good" or "bad."

If anything at all about the idea appeals to you, we urge you to give affirmations a try. Affirmations do work for many people. By affirming a good thing, you are actually reinforcing it in your life.

That's why affirmations are always expressed in completely positive terms (not, "I am not in danger," but "I am safe") and why they are expressed in present terms (not, "I will get what I want" but "I am getting what I want" or "I'm on the road I want to be on"). Affirming something completely good in the present is a way of focusing on that part of your life that *is* good, even if in your depressed state, that seems like a very small or even a nonexistent part! (For more about affirmations, see pages 46–49 in Chapter 3.)

Meditation

We've described a basic technique for meditation in Chapter 3, pages 53–54. There, we discussed it as useful for combating anxiety, but it's also extremely helpful in battling depression, as well. Like affirmations, meditation seems to be a way of centering and focusing the mind that makes room for positive thoughts and feelings as well as for a sense of power, strength, and calmness.

One Step at a Time: Setting Small Goals

One of the worst things about being depressed is that everything seems to be such an effort in that state. Other people who are not depressed may not realize how difficult it is for you even to get out of bed in the morning, let alone to clean your room or finish a homework assignment.

One of the things that may make it difficult to accomplish anything is that you are looking ahead and imagining all of the many steps that go into completing a project. If this is getting in your way, we suggest that you break tasks down into small steps, each of which is easy to imagine completing.

If you have to clean your room, for example, don't think of the entire room. Just focus on making your bed. Remind yourself that once your bed is made, you will feel differently and you can decide then what to do next. When your bed is made, allow yourself to feel a sense of accomplishment instead of immediately being overwhelmed by the six or seven tasks that you did *not* complete. Give yourself a pat on the back, reward yourself with some special treat, acknowledge that you have completed something that was actually very difficult for you. Approach schoolwork, or any other task, in the same way.

Mind Boosts

If your depressions are frequent, severe, or long-lasting, we urge you to look at Chapters 6 and 7 to explore some of the help you might get. Along with help from others, however, here are some ways you can begin to help yourself.

Put Boundaries on Your Depression

As we've said, depression seems to have the power to take over your life by feeling as though it has always been with you and always will be, as though *everything* in your life is meaningless and flat.

It may help, when you're feeling this way, to say to yourself, "This is how I feel *now. Now* I am feeling depressed." You don't have to talk yourself out of the feeling—in fact, you probably can't. But you can understand that depression is a feeling, not a reality. Putting it into a sentence that is about you and your feelings at this moment is a way of acknowledging your feelings while reminding yourself of their limits.

Feel the Feelings

Acknowledging your feeling of depression may help you to go further and look at what's really bothering you. Depression, like anxiety, is often a cover for some other feelings that seem too painful or frightening. Usually, if you can face those painful, frightening feelings, they become less frightening and you discover that you have the strength to work through them. You may be in some pain, but you won't be depressed—and sooner or later, the pain will end.

If the idea of learning more about your feelings appeals to you, try the following experiment. You may want to make yourself a tape to play with your version of the following instructions, or you may just want to refer to this book.

Find yourself a quiet, private place where you feel safe and where you won't be interrupted. Have pen and paper or drawing materials and paper ready. Shut your eyes and breathe very deeply and slowly, until you are breathing in for a count of 10 and out for a count of 10. (For more on deep breathing and how to use it to help you, see pages 50–51, Chapter 3.) Let the breath "fall in" to your body and then "fall out"—don't push or strain. Allow yourself to focus completely on your body. Notice everything you can about how you feel. If a muscle feels tight or tense, ask it to relax.

For this part of the exercise, some people enjoy picturing themselves in a completely safe and happy place, such as on a beach by the ocean or in a favorite childhood spot. Others prefer just staying aware of their bodies in *this* spot. Whichever you choose, stay with this part of the exercise until you can feel that you are relaxed and open.

Now say to yourself, "I am having an image that will teach me about my feelings." Repeat this phrase silently to yourself, and then stop. Allow an image to come into your mind. Slowly and gently, begin to observe the image that appears. Let it come into focus. Notice the details. It may start to move or change, or you may wish to ask it questions or explore it further. Find out everything you can about what you see in your mind.

When you feel that you have learned all you can, slowly open your eyes. Reach for your paper and write or draw the image that you saw. Focus on just trying to remember every detail that you can about the image that you created in your mind.

If you feel tense or excited at any point, use your deep breathing as a way of staying calm and relaxed. Center on how safe you feel in your imaginary safe place or right here inside your body.

Then go back to the image and write or draw about how it makes you feel. Be open to whatever comes out. Tell yourself ahead of time that this is about exploring yourself. You might say or write things that upset you and make you feel guilty, or you may find yourself feeling very angry, or sad, or frightened—or you may find that you are excited and exhilarated by this process or that it helps you to feel peaceful and calm. Whatever happens, find a way to stay with it until you have learned everything you can about what you imagined and how you feel about it.

Sometimes this exercise makes people feel better without knowing why. Sometimes it helps people understand something new about their lives that leads them to take action in a new way. Sometimes it brings up disturbing and upsetting feelings. Possibly, it may affect you in all three ways or in some other way. If you feel particularly disturbed or upset, again, we urge you to get help as described in Chapters 6 and 7.

Keep a Journal

Many people find it comforting to keep a journal in which they can record their private thoughts and feelings. It helps to give yourself permission to say *anything* in your journal, even feelings that you would never want to act on.

Sometimes, for example, when you are really angry with someone you love, you feel as though you hate that person. Even though you don't really hate him or her, it can be liberating to say so while you are having that feeling. A journal is a great place to do that.

Some people find it useful to record their dreams in their journal. There seems to be something soothing and centering about paying attention to your dreams in this way, even if all you do is write down what happened in them. Some people also like to go further and write about how their dreams made them feel or what they think they are telling themselves in their dreams.

Act on Your Feelings

Some feelings you can express directly to the people involved; other feelings you may choose to keep to yourself. Either way, however, you can take some kind of action.

If you're furious with a friend, teacher, or parent but don't feel comfortable yelling at that person, for example, go into your room and pound a pillow, or find a quiet place where you can yell and not be heard. Take a brisk walk and picture kicking the person with every step, until your anger has been relieved. Depression is often closely connected to anger that we are afraid to express, so finding a way to express that feeling in particular may help relieve your down times.

The important thing to remember is that you don't have to be reasonable when you are expressing your anger in private. Maybe you even understand that the other person had good reasons for doing what he or she did—but regardless, you still feel mad. If you can allow yourself to *feel* that way, and to act on it privately, however you choose to act publicly, you may find yourself feeling less depressed as well.

Of course, sometimes it is important to act on your feelings in public, as well. Girls and women seem to have an especially difficult time expressing their anger to others or expressing their wishes to do what *they* want rather than what other people want them to do. If you are frequently feeling depressed, you may want to consider whether you need to start expressing your anger and your wishes to others. Several useful books on assertiveness and on saying "no" are listed in Chapter 7. See also pages 59–60 in Chapter 3.

Reach Out

Don't stay isolated—connect. If you feel depressed, tell someone that you trust. If you don't get the help you want, don't give up—tell someone else, and keep telling people until you get the help you want. Parents, a school counselor, a religious leader, a teacher, a neighbor, or a friend might all be good people to talk to.

If Someone You Know Is Depressed

It can be very difficult to know how to handle the situation when a friend or family member is depressed. Here are some suggestions that may be helpful.

Respect Their Privacy—But Insist on Making Contact

One of the difficult things about depression is the way it leads the depressed person to become isolated from family, friends, and people in general. If someone you care about is depressed, be sure that that person knows how important it is to *you* to stay connected.

This may be difficult. The other person is likely to be pushing you away, perhaps even getting angry with you for wanting to maintain the contact. You may find yourself getting angry in response. If so, it's perfectly all right to express that anger to the person who is depressed—just express it directly, rather than by withdrawing yourself and staying away.

Here are some ways of bringing the issue up that might be useful:

"I know this is a difficult time for you, but I'm your friend and I care about you. Don't shut me out—let me in on what's going on."

"It really makes me mad that you're pushing me away like this. You're acting like I don't care about you—and I do."

"I'd just like us to spend some time together. It's OK if you're in a bad mood. You don't have to be any special way. I just like spending time with you."

Keep It in Perspective

In other words, don't take the other person's depression personally.

For many of us, this is hard to do. If someone is angry with us or seems to be rejecting us, it's easy to believe that the person is acting because we are not likable or because we have done something wrong.

Take a closer look. Is the person in question pushing away everyone who is close to him or her, choosing to spend time only with people who are more distant—or to spend time alone? In that case, the person is not responding to what's actually going on between the two of you but to his or her own depression.

Once again, it's perfectly all right to get angry about being pushed away. But it will probably be easier to feel that anger and to express it appropriately if you aren't taking the other person's actions personally.

Keep Your Own Needs in Perspective, Too

You don't have to be a victim to the feelings of the depressed person. If you have a date planned, for example, and the other person calls at the last minute to cancel because he or she is feeling too depressed to go out, you don't have to suppress all your own feelings and allow the other person's depression to run the show. You may need to express your anger and disappointment—and possibly, to find a way of staying in contact that doesn't involve making certain kinds of plans.

Likewise, if you are spending time with your friend and he or she wants to tell you that story about breaking up yet another time, you don't have to sit and listen quietly. You can say, "I've heard this story several times. I know you feel bad about breaking up with Sandy, and I feel bad for you, but I don't want to talk about it now." Or, if you are willing to listen to another depressed tale, you may want to insist on some time to talk about yourself, or to get something that you want out of the conversation.

You don't have to ignore your friend's depression or pretend that it doesn't affect your relationship with him or her. You can acknowledge that your friend is depressed and you don't have the power to cheer him or her up. But you don't have to allow that depression to rule *your* life. Once you get both your friend's needs and your needs firmly in perspective, you are free to find ways of staying connected where you don't feel abused or taken advantage of.

Tell an Adult if You Get Worried

If you become seriously worried about your friend's depression, don't try to handle it alone. Get help. Tell an adult that you trust, preferably a member of the person's family or someone who knows the person. If you can't do that, however, tell someone else—call a hot line, find a counselor, call a social service agency, or contact one of the organizations listed in Chapter 7.

Of course, if you believe your friend is contemplating suicide, you should tell someone else *immediately.* But even if you believe the situation is not that serious, you still don't have to handle it alone. Depression can be almost as hard on a person's friends and especially family as it is on the depressed person. If you are close to someone who is depressed, and particularly if you are related to the person, check out the resources for help in your community or the ones listed in Chapter 7. Just because the depressed person is isolated doesn't mean you have to be.

6

Getting Help

Throughout this book, we've urged you to get help with anxiety or depression that seems to be too intense, too frequent, too long-lasting, or just more than you can handle. Our recommendation is based on our philosophy that everyone needs help at one time or another and that finding the help you need is often the best thing you can do for yourself.

However, some people find it difficult to ask for or to accept help. Very often, the reasons that a person is feeling anxious or depressed are the very reasons that the person finds it difficult to ask for help!

With the intention of breaking this vicious cycle, we've included this chapter, to talk about why people sometimes find it difficult to reach out for help, as well as to give you some more concrete information on the kind of help that may be available for you.

What's So Hard About Asking for Help?

As we've said, often anxiety and depression come from buried feelings that a person is trying not to feel or admit to. Instinctively, that person knows that going for help—talking to a counselor, for example—increases the chances of finding out about those buried feelings. Even though releasing those feelings is ultimately the solution, sometimes it can feel like just another problem.

Lisa, for example, finally started seeing a therapist to help her with her depression. As she talked to her counselor, she discovered just how sad she felt about her parents' lack of affection for her. This was something that she had been trying to ignore for years—and now, finally, she was facing it. Naturally, it was painful.

However, what Lisa discovered, throughout the painful time, was that she was strong enough to handle it. Perhaps as a very young child, she had had to block out that reality, but now that she was older, she was not so dependent on her parents and so had more resources with which to face the truth. Lisa discovered that the very thing she had feared—facing her feelings—was actually making her stronger. Plus it was an enormous relief to be able to finally admit the truth about what she saw and what she felt!

Maria had a different experience. She was worried that if she actually expressed her feelings of anger and of sometimes wanting to put herself first, no one would like her.

Then Maria took an assertiveness class for teenagers—and suddenly the lid was off! Maria seemed always to be saying "no" to other people's requests, and she was telling people more and more easily how angry she was with them.

For a while, Maria's family and friends found it very difficult to get along with Maria. Suddenly she seemed to be acting like an angry, selfish brat. That's because all of Maria's angry feelings had been locked up for so long that they were now all coming out in a rush.

Eventually, however, as Maria got more comfortable with saying no and with feeling her feelings, she was able to handle saying "no" and saying "yes" much more easily. And Maria's family and friends had also learned to adjust to a new Maria, who wasn't quite so easy to push around. Although some of what Maria feared had come true, in the end, she had worked out a better way of getting along.

Calvin was afraid to ask for help because, as a perfectionist, he really believed that needing help meant that something was wrong with him. Since he expected himself and others to be perfect, he had to see asking for help as a sign of weakness.

When Calvin finally did speak with a sympathetic counselor, however, he realized that the very fears he had about asking for help were the fears that were getting in his way elsewhere in his life. Since his parents had not responded well to his needing help, Calvin assumed that nobody would respond well. Bottling up all his needs was making him anxious—and asking for help was a first courageous step in getting past those anxious feelings to a more realistic picture of himself. Over time, Calvin could learn that he didn't have to be perfect to be a great person; that even the "best" people sometimes need help.

Sometimes people fear asking for help because in the past, they've had bad experiences with asking for or needing help. James, for example, found that, as a child, when he asked for help, his father would get so anxious that he made James feel guilty for upsetting him. His mother would try to help by offering many possible solutions—but then James felt as though, if her solutions didn't work, he had somehow let her down. In James's experience, asking for help was just letting himself in for another set of pressures.

Tanya's experience was that asking for help opened her up to ridicule. When she would ask her older sister for advice, for example, her sister would say, "God, you're dumb. I can't believe you don't know *that*!" Naturally, Tanya learned to keep her questions to herself!

Both James and Tanya had to learn that not everyone would react the way members of their families had. In Tanya's case, she found an art teacher with whom she felt comfortable talking about her life. As Tanya was able to experience a sympathetic, interested adult whom she could trust, she could feel more comfortable about showing another side of herself.

James found a school counselor that he could talk to. Unlike his parents, James's counselor never jumped in with suggestions or advice. Instead, she asked James questions about how James felt and what James thought. James got to experience a person who gave help by focusing on him, rather than by expecting James to reassure *her* that her solutions had worked.

What Kinds of Help Are Available

Once you've decided to ask for help, what kind of help should you ask for? Here is a list that can help you decide:

Hot lines

Hot lines are telephone numbers that you can call, anonymously, to discuss various types of problems. Some hot lines focus on suicide, others on drugs and alcohol, still others on sexual abuse. Some cities have hot lines that teens can call to ask questions about gay or lesbian feelings and relationships. Many areas have general hot lines, which you can call simply to talk.

Most hot lines are open 24 hours a day, although some have more restricted hours. Hot lines are anonymous and confidential. They usually include referral services, so that if you want to ask for other sources of help, they can usually give you suggestions of where to call.

You can find hot line numbers advertised in various places. Some phone directories list them in a special section. A local social service agency might be able to tell you the hot line numbers in your community (look in the phone book under "social services," "welfare," or "family services"). There are also some national 800 numbers listed in Chapter 7 of this book. (Phone numbers with an area code of 800 are toll free.)

Support Groups

These are groups that meet to discuss various problems. Alcoholics Anonymous and all the other "anonymous" groups meet without leaders; other support groups are led by a trained counselor.

Support groups might focus on issues around food and weight, drugs, alcohol, relationships, assertiveness and expressing feelings, or just general life issues. The emphasis is on every member of the group sharing his or her experiences, without blame or judgment. Sometimes a group might offer suggestions for dealing with a problem; sometimes the group's role is simply to listen with sympathy and understanding.

Support groups are often advertised in local newspapers or on bulletin boards in bookstores, health food stores, and other community centers. Your school counselor may know of support groups in your area that would interest you. Some of the national organizations listed in Chapter 7 may know about support groups in your area as well.

Counseling

Counseling or therapy may range from talking a few times with your school counselor to seeing a psychotherapist several times a week. The focus of counseling may be a specific issue, such as helping you learn to complete work more easily, or it may be more general, such as persistent anxiety or depression. Sometimes people go to counseling for specific issues and discover that they would also benefit from talking about other problems as well.

Counseling is based on the theory that expressing a problem helps you to learn about it and to come to terms with it. In a counseling or therapy session, you'll spend most of the time talking about whatever you choose, with some questions and perhaps suggestions from your counselor. As you talk about what bothers you, you will learn something new. In addition, your counselor may suggest ways of seeing your situation that had not occurred to you.

Counselors can be especially helpful with making the switch away from some of the attitudes that we've identified as feeding anxiety and depression, helping you to focus on the positive, rather than on the negative, for example. A counselor can also be especially helpful in getting in touch with your buried feelings.

Another useful aspect of counseling is the chance it gives you for a different kind of experience. Many people in counseling have learned from their families that there is something "wrong" with them, that it isn't all right to express their needs, or that their feelings are bad and should be suppressed. A good counselor won't feel that way, and the experience of spending time with someone who sees you and the world differently can help you to also see yourself and your world in new ways.

Fees for counseling vary, as do the rules and setup for the counseling sessions. It is often possible to find free therapy or counseling, although most therapists do charge anywhere from $25 to $100 per hour for their time. If your parents are willing to pay for therapy, you have a wider range of options, but even if they are not, you may be able to get this kind of help for yourself if you are persistent. Talk to your school counselor, call a social service agency, ask a hot line for a referral (a suggestion of where else to call). If you think you would benefit from a sympathetic ear and a person with a new perspective, keep going until you find a situation that will work for you.

Family Counseling

Often, the roots of anxiety and depression are in family relationships. Therefore, sometimes it's helpful for an entire family to meet with a counselor who can help the group as a whole see new ways of working things out. Family counseling is also available through social service agencies as well as privately. Ask a teacher, counselor, or doctor for suggestions in finding a service that will work for you and your family.

What Should You Expect from Your Counseling?

Sometimes it takes time to find the counselor that is right for you. You deserve someone whom you trust, someone whom you feel respects you and cares about you. A counselor will not solve your problems for you and will probably not be available to you outside the time actually spent in a counseling session (except, of course, in an emergency). Within those limits, however, you should feel comfortable and safe talking with your counselor.

Usually, it takes some time to build up a really trusting relationship with a therapist. However, you can trust your own instincts, as well. If you see your counselor as someone whom you might someday trust, he or she is probably right for you. If you have a bad feeling about him or her from the start, you may want to look elsewhere.

It's important that you feel able to argue and disagree with your counselor. Conflicts and disagreements inevitably come up in counseling or therapy—in fact, working them out can be one of the most valuable parts of your counseling experience. So don't expect someone whom you think is perfect—that person probably doesn't exist!—but do expect someone you can talk and listen to with respect.

Anxiety and depression can be frightening emotions—but they don't have to paralyze you forever. Whether you get help from the suggestions in this book, from other people, from your own ideas, or from a combination of all three, you can find a way of coping with these conditions. As you do so, you'll discover that going through your emotions in this way has taught you something valuable about yourself, freeing you to enjoy yourself and your life in new and exciting ways.

7

Where to Find Help

The following organizations will be able to provide you with referrals and advice in dealing with a variety of problems or crises that you may have to deal with.

Alcohol and Drug Problems

Alcoholics Anonymous and World Services
468 Park Avenue South
New York, NY 10016
212-686-1100
This organization provides free referrals for those seeking recovery from alcohol problems.

Alanon Family Intergroup
200 Park Avenue South
New York, NY 10016
This service provides information and referrals for families

of alcoholics, including Alateen meetings for teenage members of an alcoholic's family.

ALCOHOL Helpline
1-800-252-6462
This organization provides counseling and referrals to treatment centers or self-help groups such as Alateen, Alanon, or Narcotics Anonymous.

Alcohol Education for Youth
1500 Western Avenue
Albany, NY 12203
514-456-3800
This educational program seeks to prevent alcohol abuse among young people, with a special emphasis on families.

Narcotics Anonymous World Service Office
16155 Wyandotte Street
Van Nuys, CA 91406
818-780-3951
This organization provides general reference services for those seeking recovery from narcotics addiction.

National Cocaine Hotline
1-800-262-2463
This service provides information and help for cocaine users, their friends, or families.

Pills Anonymous
P.O. Box 473
Ansonia Station, NY 10021
This self-help group offers support for people with drug dependency problems.

Birth Control/Family Planning

American College of Obstetrics and Gynecologists
1-800-762-2264
This service provides free brochures describing the latest, most effective methods of birth control.

If you live in one of the following states, you can call the listed numbers for additional advice, for information, and for referrals.

New Jersey: 1-800-624-2637
Illinois: 1-800-843-3228
West Virginia: 1-800-642-8522
Tennessee: 1-800-255-4936

CHOICE Hotline
215-592-0550
This help line answers teenagers' questions about birth control, pregnancy, sexually transmitted diseases, AIDS, and other related topics. Spanish operators available.

Planned Parenthood Federation of America
810 Seventh Avenue
New York, NY 10019
212-541-7800

This organization provides information on birth control, sexuality, and family life.

National Abortion Federation Hotline
1-800-772-9100
This hot line answers questions about where you can get a safe abortion.

Divorced or Single Parents

Parents Anonymous
22330 Hawthorne Blvd. (Suite 208)
Torrance, CA 90505
1-800-421-0353 (except in California)
1-800-353-0368 (California only)
This organization provides parents with self-help support (through group therapy) for prevention and treatment of child abuse. It also has programs for children from dysfunctional families.

Parents Without Partners
301-588-9354
301-648-1320
This organization provides referrals to more than 1,000 local support groups of this organization throughout the country.

Eating Disorders

American Anorexia/Bulimia Association, Inc. (AA/BA)
133 Cedar Lane
Teaneck, NJ 07666
201-836-1800

Anorexia Nervosa and Related Eating Disorders, Inc. (ANRED)
P.O. Box 5102
Eugene, OR 97405
503-344-1144

National Anorexic Aid Society, Inc. (NAAS)
550 South Cleveland Avenue, Suite F.
Westerville, OH 43081
614-436-1112

National Association of Anorexia Nervosa and Associated
    Disorders, Inc. (ANAD)
P.O. Box 271
Highland Park, IL 60035
312-831-3438

Emotional Problems

National Institutes of Mental Health
301-443-4513
This organization provides referrals for psychological counseling or therapy available in your area.

Physical and Sexual Abuse

American Humane Association
9725 East Hampden
Denver, CO 80231
303-695-0811
The American Humane Association protects children against
neglect and abuse through a variety of community service
programs.

Big Brothers-Big Sisters of America
230 North 13th Street
Philadelphia, PA 19107
215-557-8600
Big Brothers-Big Sisters provides a broad range of programs for children and teenagers, including matching children from single-parent homes with adult volunteers.

Childhelp/International
6463 Independence Avenue
Woodland Hills, CA 91370
1-800-4-A-CHILD
Childhelp provides crisis counseling information and referrals in situations dealing with child abuse.

National Center for Missing and
    Exploited Children
1835 K Street NW, Suite 700
Washington, DC 20006
1-800-843-5678

National Committee for Prevention of
    Child Abuse
332 South Michigan Avenue, Suite 1250
Chicago, IL 60604
312-663-3520

Society for the Prevention of Cruelty to
    Children
161 William Street
New York, NY 10003
212-233-5500
This organization provides referrals and counseling to families and children suffering from physical and sexual abuse.

Runaways

National Network of Runaway and Youth Services, Inc.
1400 I Street, NW (Suite 330)
Washington, DC 20005
202-682-4114
This national organization is divided into regional networks and provides services and support for families and youth at risk for child abuse, drug abuse, AIDS, and alcoholism.

The National Runaway Switchboard
1-800-621-4000
Children and teenagers who run away from home can receive referrals to hospitals, shelters, and social service agencies in their area. The Switchboard also provides a service where runaways and their families can leave messages for one another. All calls are confidential.

Suicide

Suicide Hotline Samaritans of New York
212-673-3000
This service offers suicide intervention.

Suicide Prevention 24 Hour Help line
1-800-333-4444 (Free national help line)
This service offers suicide intervention and hospital referrals.
Organizations such as the Federation of Protestant Welfare Agencies, Catholic Charities, or the Jewish Board of Family Services often have local chapters listed in the yellow pages of your telephone directory under "Social Service Organizations." They can provide information and referrals for teenagers or families in trouble.

INDEX